Jackie & Galen

Love

Mom & Dad

Hatch

I Know THAT MY REDEEMER LIVES

LATTER-DAY PROPHETS TESTIFY OF THE SAVIOR

Compiled by Heidi S. Swinton

Cover illustration: *Divine Redeemer* by Simon Dewey. Used by permission.
Art direction: Richard Erickson.
Design: Shauna Gibby. Book design © Deseret Book Company.

First Printing: First edition 1990
Published by Deseret Book Company.

Updated Edition September 2019
Published by Covenant Communications, Inc.

Printed in China

26 25 24 23 22 21 20 19 10 9 8 7 6 5 4 3 2 1

ISBN 978-1-52441-121-3

Contents

I *Know* THAT MY REDEEMER LIVES

In this last dispensation of time, the Lord Jesus Christ has called seventeen men in succession to hold the office of President of The Church of Jesus Christ of Latter-day Saints. These men are prophets, seers, and revelators. They are special witnesses of the Savior testifying clearly of His divine mission as the Savior and Redeemer of all His Father's children. Each of their testimonies—proclaimed from pulpits of Zion around the world, in the councils of the Church, in the mission field, and in their own homes—speaks of hearts and souls dedicated to the Savior and His magnificent gospel. Their words are earnest and compelling: "I know that my Redeemer lives."

I Know That My Redeemer Lives

I know that my Redeemer lives.
What comfort this sweet sentence gives!
He lives, he lives, who once was dead.
He lives, my ever-living Head.
He lives to bless me with his love.
He lives to plead for me above.
He lives my hungry soul to feed.
He lives to bless in time of need.

He lives to grant me rich supply.
He lives to guide me with his eye.
He lives to comfort me when faint.
He lives to hear my soul's complaint.

He lives to silence all my fears.
He lives to wipe away my tears.
He lives to calm my troubled heart.
He lives all blessings to impart.

He lives, my kind, wise heav'nly Friend.
He lives and loves me to the end.
He lives, and while he lives, I'll sing.
He lives, my Prophet, Priest, and King.
He lives and grants me daily breath.
He lives, and I shall conquer death.
He lives my mansion to prepare.
He lives to bring me safely there.

He lives! All glory to his name!
He lives, my Savior, still the same.
Oh, sweet the joy this sentence gives:
"I know that my Redeemer lives!"
He lives! All glory to his name!
He lives, my Savior, still the same.
Oh, sweet the joy this sentence gives:
"I know that my Redeemer lives!"
—*Hymns* (1985), no. 136

"He lives! All glory to his name!
He lives, my Savior, still the same.
Oh, sweet the joy this sentence gives:
'I know that my Redeemer lives!'"

Hymns (1985), no. 136.

1

JOSEPH SMITH JR.

First President of
The Church of Jesus Christ
of Latter-day Saints

Born
23 December 1805

Ordained an Apostle
May 1829

Years as President
1832–1844

Died
27 June 1844, age 38

This Is My Beloved Son

There was in the place where we lived an unusual excitement on the subject of religion. It commenced with the Methodists, but soon became general among all the sects in that region of country. Indeed, the whole district of country seemed affected by it, and great multitudes united themselves to the different religious parties, which created no small stir and division amongst the people. . . .

I was one day reading the Epistle of James, first chapter and fifth verse, which reads: *If any of you lack wisdom, let him ask of God, that giveth to all men liberally, and upbraideth not; and it shall be given him.*

Never did any passage of scripture come with more power to the heart of man than this did at this time to mine. It seemed to enter with great force into every feeling of my heart. I reflected on it again and again, knowing that if any person needed wisdom from God, I did; for how to act I did not know, and unless I could get more wisdom than I then had, I would never know; for the teachers of religion of the different sects understood the same passages of scripture so differently as to destroy all confidence in settling the question by an appeal to the Bible.

At length I came to the conclusion that I must either remain in darkness and confusion, or else I must do as James directs, that is, ask of God. I at length came to the determination to "ask of God," concluding that if he gave wisdom to them that lacked wisdom, and would give liberally, and not upbraid, I might venture.

So, in accordance with this, my determination to ask of God, I retired to the woods to make the attempt. It was on the morning of a beautiful, clear day, early in the spring of eighteen hundred and twenty. It was the first time in my life that I had made such an attempt, for amidst all my anxieties I had never as yet made the attempt to pray vocally.

After I had retired to the place where I had previously designed to go, having looked around me, and finding myself alone, I kneeled down and began to offer up the desires of my heart to God. I had scarcely done so, when immediately I was seized upon by some power which entirely overcame me, and had such an astonishing influence over me as to bind my tongue so that I could not speak. Thick darkness gathered around me, and it seemed to me for a time as if I were doomed to sudden destruction.

But, exerting all my powers to call upon God to deliver me out of the power of this enemy which had seized upon me, and at the very moment when I was ready to sink into despair and abandon myself to destruction—not to an imaginary ruin, but to the power of some actual being from the unseen world, who had such marvelous power as I had never before felt in any being—just at this moment of great alarm, I saw a pillar of light exactly over my head, above the brightness of the sun, which descended gradually until it fell upon me.

It no sooner appeared than I found myself delivered from the enemy which held me bound. When the light rested upon me I saw two Personages, whose brightness and glory defy all description, standing above me in the air. One of them spake unto me, calling me by name and said, pointing to the other—This is My Beloved Son. Hear Him!

My object in going to inquire of the Lord was to know which of all the sects was right, that I might know which to join. No sooner, therefore, did I get possession of myself, so as to be able to speak, than I asked the Personages who stood above me in the light, which of all the sects was right (for at this time it had never entered into my heart that all were wrong)—and which I should join.

I was answered that I must join none of them, for they were all wrong; and the Personage who addressed me said that all their creeds were an abomination in his sight; that those professors were all corrupt; that: "they draw near to me with their lips, but their hearts are far from me, they teach for doctrines the commandments of men, having a form of godliness, but they deny the power thereof."

He again forbade me to join with any of them; and many other things did he say unto me, which I cannot write at this time. When I came to myself again, I found myself lying on my back, looking up into heaven. When the light had departed, I had no strength; but soon recovering in some degree, I went home. . . .

I had actually seen a light, and in the midst of that light I saw two Personages; and they did in reality speak to me; and though I was hated and persecuted for saying that I had seen a vision, yet it was true; and while they were persecuting me, reviling me, and speaking all manner of evil against me falsely for so saying, I was led to say in my heart: Why persecute me for telling the truth? I have actually seen a vision; and who am I that I can withstand God, or why does the world think to make me deny what I have actually seen? For I had seen a vision; I knew it, and I knew that God knew it, and I could not deny it, neither dared I do it; at least I knew that by so doing I would offend God, and come under condemnation.

Joseph Smith—History 1:5, 11–20, 25.

Testimonies of Prophets

The fundamental principles of our religion are the testimony of the Apostles and Prophets, concerning Jesus Christ, that He died, was buried, and rose again the third day, and ascended into heaven; and all other things which pertain to our religion are only appendages to it. But in connection with these, we believe in the Gift of the Holy Ghost; the power of faith, the enjoyment of the spiritual gifts according to the will of God, the restoration of the house of Israel, and the final triumph of truth.

History of The Church of Jesus Christ of Latter-day Saints, *ed. B. H. Roberts, 7 vols. (Salt Lake City: The Church of Jesus Christ of Latter-day Saints, 1951), 3:30.*

When He Shall Come

When I contemplate the rapidity with which the great and glorious day of the coming of the Son of Man advances, when He shall come to receive His Saints unto Himself, where they shall dwell in His presence, and be crowned with glory and immortality; when I consider that soon the heavens are to be shaken, and the earth tremble and reel to and fro; and that the heavens are to be unfolded as a scroll when it is rolled up; and that every mountain and island are to flee away, I cry out in my heart, What manner of persons ought we to be in all holy conversation and godliness!

You remember the testimony which I bore in the name of the Lord Jesus, concerning the great work which He has brought forth in the last days. You know my manner of communication, how that in weakness and simplicity, I declared to you what the Lord had brought forth by the ministering of His holy angels to me for this generation. I pray that the Lord may enable you to treasure these things in your mind, for I know that His Spirit will bear testimony to all who seek diligently after knowledge from Him. I hope you will search the

Scriptures to see whether these things are not also consistent with those things which the ancient Prophets and Apostles have written.

History of the Church, *1:442*.

Belief in Jesus Christ

We believe in God, the Eternal Father, and in His Son, Jesus Christ, and in the Holy Ghost. . . . We believe that through the Atonement of Christ, all mankind may be saved, by obedience to the laws and ordinances of the Gospel. We believe that the first [principle] . . . of the Gospel [is]: first, Faith in the Lord Jesus Christ.

Articles of Faith 1:1, 3–4.

Vision of the Father and Son on the Throne

The heavens were opened upon us, and I beheld the celestial kingdom of God, and the glory thereof, whether in the body or out I cannot tell. I saw the transcendent beauty of the gate through which the heirs of that kingdom will enter, which was like unto circling flames of fire; also the blazing throne of God, whereon was seated the Father and the Son. I saw the beautiful streets of that kingdom, which had the appearance of being paved with gold. . . .

Thus came the voice of the Lord unto me, saying: All who have died without a knowledge of this gospel, who would have received it if they had been permitted to tarry, shall be heirs of the celestial kingdom of God; also all that shall die henceforth without a knowledge of it, who would have received it with all their hearts, shall be heirs of that kingdom; for I, the Lord, will judge all men according to their works, according to the desire of their hearts.

Doctrine and Covenants 137:1–4, 7–9.

Vision of the Lord in the Temple

In the afternoon, I assisted the other Presidents in distributing the Lord's Supper to the Church, receiving it from the Twelve, whose privilege it was to officiate at the sacred desk this day. After having performed this service to my brethren, I retired to the pulpit, the veils being dropped, and bowed myself, with Oliver Cowdery, in solemn and silent prayer. After rising from prayer, the following vision was opened to both of us. . . .

The veil was taken from our minds, and the eyes of our understanding were opened. We saw the Lord standing upon the breastwork of the pulpit, before us; and under his feet was a paved work of pure gold, in color like amber.

His eyes were as a flame of fire; the hair of his head was white like the pure snow; his countenance shone above the brightness of the sun; and his voice was as the sound of the rushing of great waters, even the voice of Jehovah, saying: I am the first and the last; I am he who liveth, I am he who was slain; I am your advocate with the Father.

Behold, your sins are forgiven you; you are clean before me; therefore, lift up your heads and rejoice. Let the hearts of your brethren rejoice, and let the hearts of all my people rejoice, who have, with their might, built this house to my name.

For behold, I have accepted this house, and my name shall be here; and I will manifest myself to my people in mercy in this house. Yea, I will appear unto my servants, and speak unto them with mine own voice, if my people will keep my commandments, and do not pollute this holy house.

Yea the hearts of thousands and tens of thousands shall greatly rejoice in consequence of the blessings which shall be poured out, and the endowment with which my servants have been endowed in this house. And the fame of this house shall spread to foreign lands; and this is the beginning of the blessing which shall be poured out upon the heads of my people. Even so. Amen.

History of the Church, *2:435; Doctrine and Covenants 110:1–10.*

"And now, after the many testimonies which have been given of him, this is the testimony, last of all, which we give of him: That he lives! For we saw him, even on the right hand of God; and we heard the voice bearing record that he is the Only Begotten of the Father—that by him, and through him, and of him, the worlds are and were created, and the inhabitants thereof are begotten sons and daughters unto God."

Doctrine and Covenants 76:22–24.

In the Name of Jesus Christ

On the morning of the 22nd of July 1839, [the Prophet] arose, reflecting upon the situation of the Saints of God in their persecutions and afflictions. He called upon the Lord in prayer, the power of God rested upon him mightily, and as Jesus healed all the sick around Him in His day, so Joseph, the Prophet of God, healed all around on this occasion. He healed all in his house and dooryard; then, in company with Sidney Rigdon and several of the Twelve, went among the sick lying on the bank of the river, where he commanded them in a loud voice, in the name of Jesus Christ, to rise and be made whole, and they were all healed. When he had healed all on the east side of the river that were sick, he and his companions crossed the Mississippi River in a ferry-boat to the west side, where we were, at Montrose. The first house they went into was President Brigham Young's. He was sick on his bed at the time. The Prophet went into his house and healed him, and they all came out together.

As they were passing by my door, Brother Joseph said: "Brother Woodruff, follow me." These were the only words spoken by any of the company from the time they left Brother Brigham's house till they crossed the public square, and entered Brother Fordham's house. Brother Fordham had been dying for an hour, and we expected each minute would be his last. I felt the spirit of God that was overpowering His Prophet. When we entered the house, Brother Joseph walked up to Brother Fordham and took him by the right hand, his left hand holding his hat. He saw that Brother Fordham's eyes were glazed, and that he was speechless and unconscious.

After taking his hand, he looked down into the dying man's face and said:

"Brother Fordham, do you not know me?"

At first there was no reply, but we all could see the effect of the spirit of God resting on the afflicted man. Joseph again spoke:

"Elijah, do you not know me?"

With a low whisper Brother Fordham answered, "Yes."

The Prophet then said:

"Have you not faith to be healed?"

The answer, which was a little plainer than before, was: "I am afraid it is too late; if you had come sooner, I think I might have been."

He had the appearance of a man waking from sleep; it was the sleep of death. Joseph then said: "Do you believe that Jesus is the Christ?"

"I do, Brother Joseph," was the response. Then the Prophet of God spoke with a loud voice as in the majesty of Jehovah:

"Elijah, I command you, in the name of Jesus of Nazareth, to arise and be made whole."

The words of the Prophet were not like the words of man, but like the voice of God. It seemed to me that the house shook on its foundation. Elijah Fordham leaped from his bed like a man raised from the dead. A healthy color came to his face, and life was manifested in every act. His feet had been done up in Indian meal poultices; he kicked these off his feet, scattered the contents, then called for his clothes and put them on. He asked for a bowl of bread and milk, and ate it. He then put on his hat and followed us into the street, to visit others who were sick.

Matthias F. Cowley, Wilford Woodruff: History of His Life and Labors *(Salt Lake City: Deseret News Press, 1909), 104–5.*

The Lord Was Not in the Thunder

The manifestations of the gift of the Holy Ghost, the ministering of angels, or the development of the power, majesty or glory of God were very seldom manifested publicly, and that generally to the people of God, as to the Israelites; but most generally when angels have come or God has revealed Himself, it has been to individuals in private, in their chamber; in the wilderness or fields, and that generally without noise or tumult. The angel delivered Peter out of prison in the dead of night; came to Paul unobserved by the rest of the crew;

appeared to Mary and Elizabeth without the knowledge of others; spoke to John the Baptist whilst the people around were ignorant of it.

When Elisha saw the chariots of Israel and the horsemen thereof, it was unknown to others. When the Lord appeared to Abraham it was at his tent door; when the angels went to Lot, no person knew them but himself, which was the case probably with Abraham and his wife; when the Lord appeared to Moses, it was in the burning bush, in the tabernacle, or in the mountain top; when Elijah was taken in a chariot of fire, it was unobserved by the world; and when he was in a cleft of a rock, there was loud thunder, but the Lord was not in the thunder; there was an earthquake, but the Lord was not in the earthquake; and then there was a still small voice, which was the voice of the Lord, saying, "What doest thou hear, Elijah?"

The Lord cannot always be known by the thunder of His voice, by the display of His glory or by the manifestation of His power; and those that are the most anxious to see these things, are the least prepared to meet them, and were the Lord to manifest His power as He did to the children of Israel, such characters would be the first to say, "Let not the Lord speak any more, lest we His people die."

History of the Church, *5:30–31*.

To Know God

It is the first principle of the gospel to know for a certainty the character, the personality, the attributes of God, and to know that we may converse with him as one man converses with another.

Teachings of the Prophet Joseph Smith *(Salt Lake City: Deseret Book Company, 1977)*, 345.

The Savior Has Been in Your Midst

At a meeting held in the Prophet's home shortly after moving to Kirtland, a twelve-year-old girl and her mother were in attendance. After prayer and singing [the Prophet] began to talk. Mary Elizabeth Lightner was sitting on a plank resting on boxes. She watched the Prophet closely.

"Suddenly he stopped speaking and seemed almost transfixed. He was looking ahead, and his face outshone the candle which was on a shelf just behind him. I thought I could almost see his cheekbones. He looked as though a search light was inside his face. After a short time he looked at us very solemnly and said, 'Brothers and Sisters do you know who has been in your midst this night?' One of the Smith family said, 'An Angel of the Lord.' Joseph did not answer. Martin Harris was sitting at the Prophet's feet on a box. He slid to his knees and said, 'I know it was the Lord and Savior Jesus Christ.' Joseph put his hand on Martin's head and answered: 'Martin, God revealed that to you. Brothers and Sisters, the Savior has been in your midst. I want you to remember it.'"

Diary of Mary Elizabeth Lightner, 4, as recorded in Ivan J. Barrett, Joseph Smith, an American Prophet: Great Moments in the Life of Joseph Smith *(Provo, Utah: Extension Publications, 1963), 15.*

The Mission of the Messiah

The spirit of Elias is first, Elijah second, and Messiah last. Elias is a forerunner to prepare the way, and the spirit and power of Elijah is to come after, holding the keys of power, building the Temple to the capstone, placing the seals of the Melchizedek Priesthood upon the house of Israel, and making all things ready; then Messiah comes to His Temple, which is last of all.

Messiah is above the spirit and power of Elijah, for He made the world, and was that spiritual rock unto Moses in the wilderness. Elijah was to come and prepare the way and build up the kingdom before the coming of the great day of the Lord, although the spirit of Elias might begin it.

I have asked of the Lord concerning His coming; and while asking the Lord, He gave a sign and said, "In the days of Noah I set a bow in the heavens as a sign and token that in any year that the bow should be seen the Lord would not come; but there should be seed time and harvest during that year; but whenever you see the bow withdrawn, it shall be a token that there shall be famine, pestilence, and great distress among the nations, and that the coming of the Messiah is not far distant."

Jesus Christ never did reveal to any man the precise time that He would come. Go and read the Scriptures, and you cannot find anything that specifies the exact hour He would come; and all that say so are false teachers.

History of the Church, 6:254.

Our Testimony, Last of All

We, Joseph Smith, Jun., and Sidney Rigdon, being in the Spirit on the sixteenth day of February, in the year of our Lord one thousand eight hundred and thirty-two—by the power of the Spirit our eyes were opened and our understandings were enlightened, so as to see and understand the things of God—even those things which were from the beginning before the world was, which were ordained of the Father, through his Only Begotten Son, who was in the bosom of the Father, even from the beginning; of whom we bear record; and the record which we bear is the fulness of the gospel of Jesus Christ, who is the Son, whom we saw and with whom we conversed in the heavenly vision.

For while we were doing the work of translation, which the Lord had appointed unto us, we came to the twenty-ninth verse of the fifth chapter of John, which was given unto us as follows—speaking of the resurrection of the dead, concerning those who shall hear the voice of the Son of Man: and shall come forth; they who have done good, in the resurrection of the just; and they who have done evil, in the resurrection of the unjust.

Now this caused us to marvel, for it was given unto us of the Spirit. And while we meditated upon these things, the Lord touched the eyes of our understandings and they were opened, and the glory of the Lord shone round about. And we beheld the glory of the Son, on the right hand of the Father, and received of his fulness; and saw the holy angels, and them who are sanctified before his throne, worshiping God, and the Lamb, who worship him forever and ever.

And now, after the many testimonies which have been given of him, this is the testimony, last of all, which we give of him: That he lives! For we saw him, even on the right hand of God; and we heard the voice bearing record that he is the Only Begotten of the Father—that by him, and through him, and of him, the worlds are and were created, and the inhabitants thereof are begotten sons and daughters unto God.

Doctrine and Covenants 76:11–24.

2

Brigham Young

BRIGHAM YOUNG

Second President of The Church of Jesus Christ of Latter-day Saints

Born
1 June 1801

Ordained an Apostle
14 February 1835

Years as President
1847–1877

Died
29 August 1877, age 76

Faith in the Son of God

Our faith is concentrated in the Son of God, and through him in the Father.

Discourses of Brigham Young, sel. John A. Widtsoe (Salt Lake City: Deseret Book Company, 1941), 26.

He Is My Master

What shall we say, will not Jesus reign and subdue the world? Is he not the Saviour of the world, and the only-begotten Son of the Father, and will he not accomplish the work he came to accomplish? Is not the earth the Lord's, the wheat, the fine flour, the gold, the silver, the earth and all its fulness? Can you imagine to yourselves anything that pertains to this earth that does not belong to its Redeemer? He is my master, my elder brother. He is the character I look to, and the one I try to serve to the best of my ability.

The Latter-day Saints believe in Jesus Christ, the only begotten Son of the Father [in the flesh], who came in the meridian of time, performed his work, suffered the penalty and paid the debt of man's original sin by offering up himself, was resurrected from the dead, and ascended to his Father; and as Jesus descended below all things, so he will ascend above all things. We believe that Jesus Christ will come again, as it is written of him: "And while they looked steadfastly toward heaven as he went up, behold two men stood by them in white apparel; which also said, Ye men of Galilee, why stand ye gazing up into heaven? this same Jesus which is taken from you into heaven, shall so come in like manner as ye have seen him go into heaven."

Discourses of Brigham Young, 26.

Jesus Is the Christ

The Latter-day Saints and every other person who is entitled to salvation, and all except those who have sinned against the Holy Ghost, may know that Jesus is the Christ in the same way that Peter knew it. Miracles do not give this knowledge to mankind, though they may serve as collateral evidence to strengthen the believer. The miracles of Jesus were known to the Jews, yet they suffered him to be put to death as a deceiver of mankind and one possessed of a devil.

Discourses of Brigham Young, 28.

He Is King of Kings

The Lord has revealed to us a plan by which we may be saved both here and hereafter. God has done everything we could ask, and more than we could ask. The errand of Jesus to earth was to bring his brethren and sisters back into the presence of the Father; he has done his part of the work, and it remains for us to do ours. There is not one thing that the Lord could do for the salvation of the human family that he has neglected to do; and it remains for the children of men to receive the truth or reject it; all that can be accomplished for their salvation, independent of them, has been accomplished in and by the Savior. . . .

He is now King of kings and Lord of lords, and the time will come when every knee will bow and every tongue confess to the glory of God the Father, that Jesus is the Christ. That very character that was looked upon, not as the Savior, but as an outcast, who was crucified between two thieves and treated with scorn and derision, will be greeted by all men as the only Being through whom they can obtain salvation.

Discourses of Brigham Young, *27.*

A Glorious Resurrection

Jesus came to establish his spiritual kingdom, or to introduce a code of morals that would exalt the spirits of the people to godliness and to God, that they might thereby secure to themselves a glorious resurrection and a title to reign on the earth when the kingdoms of this world should become the kingdoms of our God and his Christ. He also came to introduce himself as the Savior of the world, to shed his blood upon the altar of atonement, and open up the way of life to all believers.

Deseret News Weekly, *13 August 1862.*

He Is Master of the Resurrection

Jesus is the first begotten from the dead, as you will understand. Neither Enoch, Elijah, Moses nor any other man that ever lived on earth, no matter how strictly he lived, ever obtained a resurrection until after Jesus Christ's body was called from the tomb by the angel. He was the first begotten from the dead. He is the Master of the resurrection—the first flesh that lived here after receiving the glory of the resurrection.

Discourses of Brigham Young, *374.*

He Has All Power

This was no miracle to him. He had the issues of life and death in his power; he had power to lay down his life and power to take it up again. This is what he says, and we must believe this if we believe the history of the Savior and the sayings of the Apostles recorded in the New Testament. Jesus had this power in and of himself; the Father bequeathed it to him; it was his legacy.

Discourses of Brigham Young, *340–41*.

He Died for Us

It is one of the greatest blessings we could enjoy, to come before the Lord, and before the angels, and before each other, to witness that we remember that the Lord Jesus Christ has died for us. This proves to the Father that we remember our covenants, that we love his Gospel, that we love to keep his commandments, and to honor the name of the Lord Jesus Christ upon the earth.

Discourses of Brigham Young, *172*.

Laboring with Him

No man will be saved and come into the presence of the Father, only through the Gospel of Jesus Christ—the same for one as the other. The Lord has his cause, his ways, his work; he will finish it up. Jesus is laboring with his might to sanctify and redeem the earth and to bring back his brethren and sisters into the presence of the Father. We are laboring with him for the purification of the whole human family, that we and they may be prepared to dwell with God in his Kingdom.

Discourses of Brigham Young, *389*.

He Is the Good Shepherd

How are we to know the voice of the Good Shepherd from the voice of a stranger? Can any person answer this question? I can. It is very easy. To every philosopher upon the earth, I say, your eye can be deceived, so can mine; your ear can be deceived, so can mine; the touch of your hand can be deceived, so can mine; but the Spirit of God filling the creature with revelation and the light of eternity, cannot be mistaken—the revelation which comes from God is never mistaken. When an individual, filled with the Spirit of God, declares the truth of heaven, the sheep hear that, the Spirit of the Lord pierces their inmost souls and sinks deep into their hearts; by the testimony of the Holy Ghost light springs up within them, and they see and understand for themselves.

Discourses of Brigham Young, *431*.

He Asks Us to Be Honest

And if we accept salvation on the terms it is offered to us, we have got to be honest in every thought, in our reflections, in our meditations, in our private circles, in our deals, in our declarations, and in every act of our lives, fearless and regardless of every principle of error, of every principle of falsehood that may be presented.

Discourses of Brigham Young, *389*.

A Testimony of Jesus Is a Privilege

It is the privilege of all to have the testimony of Jesus—to have the Spirit of prophecy. I have no greater privilege to enjoy the Spirit of prophecy than you have. I have no better right to the Holy Ghost than you. If you will live as you are taught, you will walk in darkness no more, but will walk in the light of life.

Deseret News Weekly, *5 April 1860*.

The Church Is True

I can bear testimony that the gospel of Jesus Christ is true; and the word of the Lord, whether written or spoken, is true.

Deseret News Weekly, *4 September 1852*.

Jesus Is the Savior and Redeemer of the World

I testify that Jesus is the Christ, the Saviour and Redeemer of the world; I have obeyed His sayings, and realized His promise, and the knowledge I have of Him, the wisdom of this world cannot give, neither can it take away.

Deseret News Weekly, *11 October 1876.*

Witness within Us

You and I must have the testimony of Jesus within us, or it is of but little use for us to pretend to be servants of God. We must have that living witness within us.

Discourses of Brigham Young, *430.*

The Priesthood of God

If anybody wants to know what the Priesthood of the Son of God is, it is the law by which the worlds are, were, and will continue for ever and ever. It is that system which brings worlds into existence and peoples them, gives them their revolutions—their days, weeks, months, years, their seasons and times and by which they are rolled up as a scroll, as it were, and go into a higher state of existence.

Discourses of Brigham Young, *130.*

A Perfect Order

The Priesthood of the Son of God, which we have in our midst, is a perfect order and system of government, and this alone can deliver the human family from all the evils which now afflict its members, and insure them happiness and felicity hereafter.

Discourses of Brigham Young, *130.*

"I testify that Jesus is the Christ, the Saviour and Redeemer of the world; I have obeyed His sayings, and realized His promise, and the knowledge I have of Him, the wisdom of this world cannot give, neither can it take away."

Deseret News Weekly,
11 October 1876.

The Priesthood

The Lord Almighty will not suffer his Priesthood to be again driven from the earth.

Discourses of Brigham Young, *131*.

The Kingdom of God on Earth

In the setting forth of items of doctrine which pertain to the progress and further building up of the Kingdom of God upon the earth, and the revealing of his mind and will, he has but one mouth through which to make known his will to his people. When the Lord wishes to give a revelation to his people, when he wishes to reveal new items of doctrine to them, or administer chastisement, he will do it through the man whom he has appointed to that office and calling. The rest of the offices and callings of the Church are helps and governments for the edifying of the body of Christ and the perfection of the Saints, etc., every president, bishop, elder, priest, teacher, deacon and member standing in his order and officiating in his standing and degree of Priesthood as ministers of the words of life as shepherds to watch over departments and sections of the flock of God in all the world, and as helps to strengthen the hands of the Presidency of the whole Church.

Discourses of Brigham Young, *137*.

When Worshipping

When people assemble to worship they should leave their worldly cares where they belong, then their minds are in a proper condition to worship the Lord, to call upon him in the name of Jesus, and to get his Holy Spirit, that they may hear and understand things as they are in eternity, and know how to comprehend the providences of our God. This is the time for their minds to be open, to behold the invisible things of God, that he reveals by his Spirit.

Discourses of Brigham Young, *167*.

Immortal Truths

The Lord has planted within us a divinity; and that divine immortal spirit requires to be fed. Will earthly food answer for that purpose? No; it will only keep this body alive as long as the spirit stays with it, which gives us an opportunity of doing good. That divinity within us needs food from the Fountain from which it emanated. It is not of the earth, earthy, but is from heaven. Principles of eternal life, of God and godliness, will alone feed the immortal capacity of man and give true satisfaction.

Discourses of Brigham Young, *165.*

We Are the Lord's

We are not our own, we are bought with a price, we are the Lord's; our time, our talents, our gold and silver, our wheat and fine flour, our wine and our oil, our cattle, and all there is on this earth that we have in our possession is the Lord's, and he requires one-tenth of this for the building up of his Kingdom. Whether we have much or little, one-tenth should be paid in for tithing.

Discourses of Brigham Young, *176.*

The Open Gate

The gospel of Jesus Christ is the opening avenue—the open gate in the road or way from earth to heaven, through which direct revelation comes to the children of men in their various capacities, according to their callings and standing in the society in which they live. The gospel of salvation is a portion of the law that pertains to the kingdom where God resides.

Deseret News Weekly, *19 September 1860.*

The Greatest Gift

Those who are faithful will continue to increase, and this is the great blessing the Lord has given to, or placed within the reach of the children of man, even to be capable of receiving eternal lives. . . . To have such a promise so sealed upon our heads, which no power on earth, in heaven, or beneath the earth can take it from us, to be sealed up to the day of redemption and have the promise of eternal lives, is the greatest gift of all.

Deseret News Weekly, *20 June 1855.*

The Salt Lake Temple

If the inquiry is in the hearts of the people—"Does the Lord require the building of a temple at our hands?" I can say that He requires it just as much as ever He required one to be built elsewhere. If you should ask, "Brother Brigham, have you any knowledge concerning this? Have you ever had a revelation from heaven upon it?" I can answer truly, it is before me all the time, not only today, but it was almost five years ago, when we were on this ground, looking for locations, sending our scouting parties through the country, to the right and to the left, to the north and the south, to the east and the west; before we had any returns from any of them, I knew, just as well as I now know, that this was the ground on which to erect a temple—it was before me.

The Lord wished us to gather to this place, He wished us to cultivate the earth, and make these valleys like the Garden of Eden, and make all the improvements in our power, and build a temple as soon as circumstances would permit. And further, if the people and the Lord required it, I would give a written revelation, but let the people do the things they know to be right.

14 February 1853, Journal of Discourses, *26 vols. (London: Latter-day Saints' Book Depot, 1855–86), 1:277.*

Why We Build Temples

It may be asked why we build temples. We build temples because there is not a house on the face of the whole earth that has been reared to God's name which will in anywise compare with his character, and that he can consistently call his house. There are places on the earth where the Lord can come and dwell, if he pleases. They may be found on the tops of high mountains, or in some cavern or places where sinful man has never marked the soil with his polluted feet.

Discourses of Brigham Young, *393–94.*

A House of God

He requires his servants to build him a house that he can come to and where he can make known his will.

Discourses of Brigham Young, *394.*

A Spiritual Eye

I testify that there is a God and that Jesus Christ lives, and that He is the Saviour of the world. Have you been to heaven and learned to the contrary? I know that Joseph Smith was a prophet of God, and that he had many revelations. Who can disprove this testimony? Any one may dispute it, but there is no one in the world who can disprove it. I have had many revelations; I have seen and heard for myself, and know these things are true, and nobody on earth can disprove them. The eye, the ear, the hand, all the senses may be deceived, but the Spirit of God cannot be deceived; and when inspired with that Spirit the whole man is filled with knowledge, he can see with a spiritual eye and he knows [that which is] beyond the power of man to controvert. What I know concerning God, concerning the earth, concerning government, I have received from the heavens not alone through my natural ability, and I give God the glory and the praise.

Deseret News Weekly, *11 June 1873.*

A Perfect Oneness

The Savior sought continually to impress upon the minds of His disciples that a perfect oneness reigned among all celestial beings—that the Father and the

"I testify that there is a God and that Jesus Christ lives, and that He is the Saviour of the world. Have you been to heaven and learned to the contrary? I know that Joseph Smith was a prophet of God, and that he had many revelations. Who can disprove this testimony? Any one may dispute it, but there is no one in the world who can disprove it. I have had many revelations; I have seen and heard for myself, and know these things are true, and nobody on earth can disprove them."

Deseret News Weekly, 11 June 1873.

Son and their Minister, the Holy Ghost, were one in their administration in heaven and among the people pertaining to this earth . . . If the heavenly hosts were not one, they would be entirely unfit to dwell . . . with the Father and Ruler of the universe.

Discourses of Brigham Young, *282*.

Be One

If we were one, we should then prove to heaven, to God our Father, to Jesus Christ our Elder Brother, to the angels, to the good upon the earth, and to all mankind that we are the disciples of the Lord Jesus Christ. If we are not one, we are not in the true sense of the word the disciples of the Lord Jesus.

Discourses of Brigham Young, *281*.

We Look Forward

We look forward to the day when the Lord will prepare for the building of the New Jerusalem, preparatory to the City of Enoch's going to be joined with it when it is built upon this earth. We are anticipating to enjoy that day, whether we sleep in death previous to that, or not. We look forward, with all the anticipation and confidence that children can possess in a parent, that we shall be there when Jesus comes; and if we are not there, we will come with him: in either case we shall be there when he comes.

Discourses of Brigham Young, *120*.

3

JOHN TAYLOR

Third President of The Church of Jesus Christ of Latter-day Saints

Born
1 November 1808

Ordained an Apostle
19 December 1838

Years as President
1880–1887

Died
25 July 1887, age 78

Trust in the Lord

I would rather trust in the living God than in any other power on earth.

Deseret News Semi-Weekly, *10 June 1884.*

Dignity of a God

A man, as a man, could arrive at all the dignity that a man was capable of obtaining or receiving; but it needed a God to raise him to the dignity of a God.

Mediation and Atonement of Our Lord and Savior Jesus Christ *(Salt Lake City: Deseret News Company, 1882; 1975 reprint), 145.*

Christ Is Our Life

I don't believe in meeting Christ at death. I believe that Christ is our life and that when he who is our life shall appear, we shall appear like unto him in glory; he is our life, our living head, and by the power that dwells in him, we may be raised to immortal bloom, and grasp eternity itself. . . . We can look unto Jesus Christ, forever. We can do the works that he did, and greater; because he has gone to the Father, for we are told, all things were created by him, and for him; principalities, powers, things present, and things to come; and if ever we should get to such a state, as to be like him we might be able to do such kind of business as he did; . . . Jesus was not prepared to govern, till he was placed in circumstances that gave him experience. The scriptures say, it is necessary to the bringing of many souls to glory, that the Captain of our salvation should be made perfect [through] sufferings. So, he was not perfect before, but he had to come here to be made perfect; he had to come here to pass through a multitude of sufferings, and be tempted and tried in all points like unto us, because it was necessary. Had it not been necessary he would not have been placed in those circumstances, and this is the reason why we are here, and kicked and cuffed round, and hated and despised, by the world. The reason why we do not live in peace is because we are not prepared for it. We are tempted and tried, driven, mobbed, and robbed; apostates are in our midst, which cause trouble and vexation of spirit, and it is all to keep down our pride and learn us to honor the God of Jacob in all things and to make us appear what we really are.

Millennial Star *(1846), 87.*

Praise the Lord

Who made this earth? The Lord. Who sustains it? The Lord. Who feeds and clothes the millions of the human family that exist upon it, both Saint and sinner? The Lord. Who upholds everything in the universe? The Lord. Who provides for the myriads of cattle, fish, and fowl that inhabit the sea, earth, and air? The Lord. Who has implanted in them that instinct which causes them to take care of their young, and that power by which to propagate their species? The Lord. Who has given to man understanding? The Lord. Who has given to the Gentile philosopher, machinist, &c., every particle of intelligence they have with regard to the electric telegraph, the power and application of steam to the wants of the human family, and every kind of invention that has been brought to light during the last century? The Lord. Who sets up the kings, emperors, and potentates that rule and govern the universe? The Lord. And who is there that acknowledges his hand? Where is the nation, the people, the church even, or other power that does it? You may wander east, west, north, and south, and you cannot find it in any church or government on the earth, except the Church of Jesus Christ of Latter-day Saints.

Deseret News Weekly, *11 November 1857.*

The Glory Be Thine

At [the] Council in the heavens the plan that should be adopted in relation to the sons of God who were then spirits, and had not yet obtained tabernacles, was duly considered. For, in view of the creation of the world and the placing of men upon it, whereby it would be possible for them to obtain tabernacles, and in those tabernacles obey laws of life, and with them again be exalted among the Gods, we are told, that at that time, "the morning stars sang together, and all the sons of God shouted for joy." The question then arose, how, and upon what principle, should the salvation, exaltation and eternal glory of God's sons be brought about?

It is evident that at that Council certain plans had been proposed and discussed, and that after a full discussion of those principles, and the declaration of the Father's will pertaining to His design, Lucifer came before the Father, with a plan of his own, saying, "Behold, [here am] I, send me, I will be thy Son, and I will redeem all mankind, that one soul shall not be lost, and surely I will do it; wherefore, give me thine honor." But Jesus, on hearing this statement made by Lucifer, said, "Father, thy will be done, and the glory be thine forever."

From these remarks made by the well beloved Son, we should naturally infer that in the discussion of this subject the Father had made known His will and developed His plan and design pertaining to these matters, and all that

His well beloved Son wanted to do was to carry out the will of His Father, as it would appear had been before expressed. He also wished the glory to be given to His Father, who, as God the Father, and the originator and designer of the plan, had a right to all the honor and glory.

But Lucifer wanted to introduce a plan contrary to the will of his Father, and then wanted His honor, and said: "I will save every soul of man, wherefore give me thine honor." He wanted to go contrary to the will of his Father, and presumptuously sought to deprive man of his free agency, thus making him a serf, and placing him in a position in which it was impossible for him to obtain that exaltation which God designed should be man's, through obedience to the law which He had suggested; and again, Lucifer wanted the honor and power of his Father, to enable him to carry out principles which were contrary to the Father's wish.

Mediation and Atonement, 93–94.

The Father's Plan

[Lucifer's] plan . . . was rejected as contrary to the counsel of God, his Father. The well beloved Son then addressed the Father, and instead of proposing to carry out any plan of His own, knowing what His Father's will was, said, "Thy will be done; I will carry out thy plans and thy designs, and, as man will fall, I will offer myself as an atonement according to thy will, O God. Neither do I wish the honor, but thine be the glory;" and a covenant was entered into between Him and His Father, in which He agreed to atone for the sins of the world, and He thus, as stated, became the Lamb slain from before the foundation of the world.

Mediation and Atonement, 97.

Eternal Life and Exaltation

Through the great atonement, the expiatory sacrifice of the Son of God, it is made possible that man can be redeemed, restored, resurrected and exalted to the elevated position designed for him in the creation as a Son of God: that eternal justice and law required the penalty to be paid by man himself, or by the atonement of the Son of God: that Jesus offered Himself as the great expiatory sacrifice; that this offering being in accordance with the demands or requirements of the law, was accepted by the great Lawgiver; that it was prefigured by sacrifices, and ultimately fulfilled by Himself according to the eternal covenant. "He was wounded [as prophesied of] for our transgressions, he was bruised for our iniquities, the chastisement of our peace was upon him, and with his stripes we are healed."

The Savior thus becomes master of the situation—the debt is paid, the redemption made, the covenant fulfilled, justice satisfied, the will of God done, and all power is now given into the hands of the Son of God—the power of the resurrection, the power of the redemption, the power of salvation, the power to enact laws for the carrying out and accomplishment of this design. Hence life and immortality are brought to light, the Gospel is introduced, and He becomes the author of eternal life and exaltation, He is the Redeemer, the Resurrector, the Savior of man and the world; and He has appointed the law of the Gospel as the medium which must be complied with in this world or the next, as He complied with His Father's law; hence "he that believeth shall be saved, and he that believeth not shall be damned."

The plan, the arrangement, the agreement, the covenant was made, entered into and accepted before the foundation of the world; it was prefigured by sacrifices, and was carried out and consummated on the cross.

Hence being the mediator between God and man, He becomes by right the dictator and director on earth and in heaven for the living and for the dead, for the past, the present and the future, pertaining to man as associated with this earth or the heavens, in time or eternity, the Captain of our salvation, the Apostle and High-Priest of our profession, the Lord and Giver of life.

Mediation and Atonement, *170–71*.

He Descended below All

As a God, He descended below all things, and made Himself subject to man in man's fallen condition; as a man, He grappled with all the circumstances incident to His sufferings in the world. Anointed, indeed, with the oil of gladness above His fellows, He struggled with and overcame the powers of men and devils, of earth and hell combined; and aided by this superior power of the Godhead, He vanquished death, hell and the grave, and arose triumphant as the Son of God, the very eternal Father, the Messiah, the Prince of peace, the Redeemer, the Savior of the world; having finished and completed the work pertaining to the atonement, which His Father had given Him to do as the Son of God and the Son of man. As the Son of man, He endured all that it was possible for flesh and blood to endure; as the Son of God He triumphed over all, and forever ascended to the right hand of God.

Mediation and Atonement, *149–51*.

The First Born

He, in the nearness of His relationship to the Father, seems to occupy a position that no other person occupies. He is spoken of as His well beloved Son, as the Only Begotten of the Father—does not this mean the only begotten after the flesh? If He was the first born and obedient to the laws of His Father, did He not inherit the position by right to be the representative of God, the Savior and Redeemer of the world? And was it not His peculiar right and privilege as the firstborn, the legitimate heir of God, the Eternal Father, to step forth, accomplish and carry out the designs of His Heavenly Father pertaining to the redemption, salvation and exaltation of man? And being Himself without sin (which no other mortal was), He took the position of Savior and Redeemer, which by right belonged to Him as the first born. And does it not seem that in having a body specially prepared, and being the offspring of God, both in body and spirit, He stood preeminently in the position of the Son of God, or in the

"I know that God rules and reigns in this nation and among the nations of the earth, and that He will direct all things, according to the counsels of His will. I know that the work that God has commenced in these last days will continue to go forth despite the powers of darkness and all the fiends of hell."

Deseret News Weekly, 17 September 1884.

place of God, and was God, and was thus the fit and only personage capable of making an infinite atonement?

Mediation and Atonement, *136–37*.

Bear Our Weaknesses and Infirmities

It is necessary, then, that we pass through the school of suffering, trial, affliction, and privation, to know ourselves, to know others, and to know our God. Therefore it was necessary, when the Saviour was upon the earth, that he should be tempted in all points, like unto us, and "be touched with the feeling of our infirmities," to comprehend the weaknesses and strength, the perfections and imperfections of poor fallen human nature. And having accomplished the thing he came into the world to do; having had to grapple with the hypocrisy, corruption, weakness, and imbecility of man; having met with temptation and trial in all its various forms, and overcome, he has become a "faithful High Priest" to intercede for us in the everlasting kingdom of his Father. He knows how to estimate and put a proper value upon human nature, for he having been placed in the same position as we are, knows how to bear with our weaknesses and infirmities, and can fully comprehend the depth, power, and strength of the afflictions and trials that men have to cope with in this world, and thus understandingly and by experience, he can bear with them as a father and an elder brother.

It is necessary, also, inasmuch as we profess that we are aiming at the same glory, exaltation, power, and blessings in the eternal world, that we should pass through the same afflictions, endure the same privations, conquer as he conquered, and overcome as he did, and thus by integrity, truth, virtue, purity, and a high-minded and honorable course before God, angels, and men, secure for ourselves an eternal exaltation in the eternal world, as he did.

12 June 1853, Journal of Discourses, *1:148*.

Infinite Atonement

We are told in . . . the Book of Mormon that the atonement must needs be infinite. Why did it need an infinite atonement? For the simple reason that a stream can never rise higher than its fountain; and man having assumed a fleshly body and become of the earth earthy, and through the violation of a law having cut himself off from his association with his Father, and become subject to death; in this condition, as the mortal life of man was short, and in and of himself he could have no hope of benefitting himself, or redeeming himself from his fallen condition, or of bringing himself back to the presence of his Father, some superior agency was needed to elevate him above his low and degraded position. This superior agency was the Son of God, who had not, as man had, violated a law of His Father, but was yet one with His Father, possessing His glory, His power, His authority, His dominion.

Mediation and Atonement, *145.*

The Just and the Unjust

If it were not for the atonement of Jesus Christ, the sacrifice he made, all the human family would have to lie in the grave throughout eternity without any hope. But God having provided, through the atonement of the Lord Jesus Christ, the medium whereby we can be restored to the bosom and presence of the Father, to participate with him among the Gods in the eternal worlds—he having provided for that, has also provided for the resurrection. He proclaimed himself the resurrection and the life. Said he, "I am the resurrection, and the life: he that believeth in me, though he were dead, yet shall he live." (John 11:25.) By and by the tombs will be opened and the dead will hear the voice of the Son of God, and they shall come forth, they who have done good to the resurrection of the just, and they who have done evil to the resurrection of the unjust.

The Gospel Kingdom: Selections from the Writings and Discourses of John Taylor*, sel. G. Homer Durham (Salt Lake City: Deseret Book Company, 1943), 118.*

The Living and the Dead

And this provision [the Atonement] applies not only to the living, but also to the dead, so that all men who have existed in all ages, who do exist now, or who will exist while the earth shall stand, may be placed upon the same footing, and that all men may have the privilege, living or dead, of accepting the conditions of the great plan of redemption provided by the Father, through the Son, before the world was; and that the justice and mercy of God may be applied to every being, living or dead, that ever has existed, that does now exist, or that ever will exist.

Mediation and Atonement, *181*.

The Pattern of Heavenly Things

This church has the seeds of immortality in its midst. It is not of man, nor by man—it is the offspring of Deity: it is organized after the pattern of heavenly things, through the principles of revelation; by the opening of the heavens, by the ministering of angels, and the revelations of Jehovah. It is not affected by the death of one or two, or fifty individuals; it possesses a priesthood after the order of Melchisedec, having the power of an endless life, "without beginning of days, or end of years." It is organized for the purpose of saving this generation, and generations that are past; it exists in time and will exist in eternity. This church fail? No! Times and seasons may change, revolution may succeed revolution, thrones may be cast down, and empires be dissolved, earthquakes may rend the earth from centre to circumference, the mountains may be hurled out of their places, and the mighty ocean be moved from its bed; but amidst the crash of worlds and crack of matter, truth, eternal truth, must remain unchanged, and those principles which God has revealed to his Saints be unscathed amidst the warring elements, and remain as firm as the throne of Jehovah.

Times and Seasons, *15 December 1844*.

Despite the Darkness

I know that God rules and reigns in this nation and among the nations of the earth, and that He will direct all things, according to the counsels of His will. I know that the work that God has commenced in these last days will continue to go forth despite the powers of darkness and all the fiends of hell.

Deseret News Weekly, *17 September 1884.*

One of the Godhead

He is the brightness of His Father's glory and the express image of His person. Also, He doeth what He seeth the Father do, while we only do that which we are permitted and empowered to do by Him. He is the Elect, the chosen, and one of the Presidency in the heavens, and in Him dwells all the fullness of the Godhead bodily, which not be said of us in any of these particulars. Another thing is, that all power is given to Him in heaven and upon earth, which no earthly being could say.

Mediation and Atonement, *136.*

In the Name of the Son

"His name shall be called Immanuel," which being interpreted is, God with us. Hence He is not only called the Son of God, the First Begotten of the Father, the Well Beloved, the Head, and Ruler, and Dictator of all things, Jehovah, the I Am, the Alpha and Omega, but He is also called the Very Eternal Father. Does not this mean that in Him were the attributes and power of the Very Eternal Father? For the angel to Adam said that all things should be done in His name. A voice was heard from the heavens, when Jesus was baptized by John the Baptist, saying, "This is my beloved Son, in whom I am well pleased," and when the Father and the Son appeared together to the Prophet Joseph Smith they were exactly alike in form, in appearance, in glory; and the Father said, pointing to His Son. "This is my beloved Son; hear Him." There the Father had

"I pray God the Eternal Father that when we have all finished our probation here, we may be presented to the Lord without spot or blemish, as pure and honorable representatives of the Church and kingdom of God on the earth, and then inherit a celestial glory in the kingdom of our God."

The Life of John Taylor, 398.

His apparent tabernacle, and the Son had His apparent tabernacle; but the Son was the agency through which the Father would communicate to man; as it is elsewhere said, "Wherefore, thou shalt do all that thou doest in the name of the Son. And thou shalt repent, and shalt call upon God, in the name of the Son, for evermore."

Mediation and Atonement, *138.*

As Honorable Representatives

I pray God the Eternal Father that when we have all finished our probation here, we may be presented to the Lord without spot or blemish, as pure and honorable representatives of the Church and kingdom of God on the earth, and then inherit a celestial glory in the kingdom of our God, and enjoy everlasting felicity with the pure and just in the realms of eternal day, through the merits and atonement of the Lord Jesus Christ, our Savior and Redeemer, in worlds without end. Amen.

B. H. Roberts, The Life of John Taylor *(Salt Lake City: Bookcraft, 1963), 398.*

4

WILFORD WOODRUFF

Fourth President of The Church of Jesus Christ of Latter-day Saints

Born
1 March 1807

Ordained an Apostle
26 April 1839

Years as President
1889–1998

Died
2 September 1898, age 91

At the Head of the Church

God has led this Church from the beginning, by prophets and inspired men. He will lead this Church until the scene is wound up.

Deseret Weekly, *5 September 1891.*

The Mind and Will of God

The Lord has taught us . . . that it matters not whether he speaks from the heavens by his own voice, or by the ministration of angels, or by the mouth of his servants when they are moved upon by the Holy Ghost, it is all the same, the mind and will of God.

Deseret News Semi-Weekly, *26 March 1878.*

A Great Blessing

We have the privilege of walking in the light, we have the privilege of comprehending and knowing the truth, of knowing the way to be saved and exalted in the presence of our Father and God. We are in a position to know his mind and will, through his servants the prophets. The Lord has given unto us teachers and inspired men, men who are inspired by the Spirit and power of God; clothed them with truth and endowed them with wisdom to teach us at all times the path we should walk in. This is a great blessing.

Deseret News, *26 December 1860.*

Priesthood Keys

I am the only man living in the flesh that received endowments under the hands of the Prophet Joseph Smith. I am the only man in the flesh that was with the Twelve Apostles when he turned over the kingdom of God to them and laid upon them the commandment to bear off this kingdom. He stood for some three hours in a room delivering to us his last lecture. The room was filled as with consuming fire. His face was as clear as amber; his words were like vivid lightning to us. They penetrated every part of our bodies from the crown of our head to the soles of our feet. He said, "Brethren, the Lord Almighty has sealed upon my head every Priesthood, every key, every power, every principle that belongs to the last dispensation of the fulness of times, and to the building up of the kingdom of God. I have sealed upon your heads all those principles, Priesthood, apostleship, and keys of the kingdom of God, and now you have got to round up your shoulders and bear off this kingdom or you will be damned." I do not forget those words—I never shall while I live. That was the last speech he ever made in the flesh. Soon afterward he was martyred and called home to glory.

Deseret News Weekly, *4 September 1897.*

Redemption from Eternal Death

It [has] been fully established beyond all controversy, from the flood of testimony . . . from the revelations of God, given in various dispensations and ages of the world, and in different parts of the globe, that the object of Christ's mission to the earth was to offer himself as a sacrifice to redeem mankind from eternal death, and that it was perfectly in accordance with the will of the Father that such a sacrifice should be made. He acted strictly in obedience to his Father's will in all things from the beginning, and drank of the bitter cup given him. Herein is brought to light, glory, honour, immortality, and eternal life, with that charity which is greater than faith or hope, for the Lamb of God has thereby performed that for man which [man] could not accomplish for himself.

Deseret News Semi-Weekly, *11 August 1868.*

Saving Souls

There is no being that has power to save the souls of men and give them eternal life, except the Lord Jesus Christ, under the command of His Father.

The Discourses of Wilford Woodruff, *ed. G. Homer Durham (Salt Lake City: Bookcraft, 1946), 23.*

Five Wise and Five Foolish Saints

The parable of the ten virgins is intended to represent the second coming of the Son of Man, the coming of the Bridegroom to meet the bride, the Church, the Lamb's wife, in the last days; and I expect that the Savior was about right when he said, in reference to the members of the Church, that five of them were wise and five were foolish; for when the Lord of heaven comes in power and great glory to reward every man according to the deeds done in the body, if he finds one-half of those professing to be members of his Church prepared for salvation, it will be as many as can be expected, judging by the course that many are pursuing.

The Discourses of Wilford Woodruff, *254.*

The Testimony of the Holy Ghost

What is the greatest testimony any man or woman can have as to this being the work of God? I will tell you what is the greatest testimony I have ever had, the most sure testimony, that is the testimony of the Holy Ghost, the testimony of the Father and the Son. We may have the ministration of angels; we may be wrapt in the visions of heaven—these things as testimonies are very good, but when you receive the Holy Ghost, when you receive the testimony of the Father and the Son, it is a true principle to every man on earth, it deceives no man, and by that principle you can learn and understand the mind of God. Revelation has been looked upon by this Church, as well as by the world, as something very marvelous. What is revelation? The testimony of the Father and Son. How many of you have had revelation? How many of you have had the Spirit of God whisper unto you—the still small voice. I would have been in the spirit world a great many years ago, if I had not followed the promptings of the still small voice. These were the revelations of Jesus Christ, the strongest testimony a man or a woman can have. I have had many testimonies since I have been connected with this Church and kingdom. I have been blessed at times with certain gifts and graces, certain revelations and ministrations; but with them all I have never found anything that I could place more dependence upon than the still small voice of the Holy Ghost.

3 July 1880, Journal of Discourses, *21:195–96.*

Baptism for the Dead Revealed

It appeared to me that the God who revealed that principle unto man was wise, just and true, possessed both the best of attributes and good sense and knowledge. I felt he was consistent with both love, mercy, justice and judgment, and I felt to love the Lord more than ever before in my life. . . . I felt to say hallelujah when the revelation came forth revealing to us baptism for the dead. I felt that we had a right to rejoice in the blessings of Heaven.

Deseret News, *27 May 1857.*

"There is no being that has power to save the souls of men and give them eternal life, except the Lord Jesus Christ, under the command of His Father."

The Discourses of Wilford Woodruff, 23.

Temples for the Savior's Work

This is a preparation necessary for the second advent of the Savior; and when we shall have built the temples now contemplated, we will then begin to see the necessity of building others, for in proportion to the diligence of our labors in this direction, will we comprehend the extent of the work to be done, and the present is only a beginning. When the Savior comes, a thousand years will be devoted to this work of redemption; and temples will appear all over this land of Joseph—North and South America—and also in Europe and elsewhere; and all the descendants of Shem, Ham, and Japheth, who received not the gospel in the flesh, must be officiated for in the Temples of God, before the Savior can present the kingdom to the Father, saying, "It is finished."

16 September 1877, Journal of Discourses, *19:229–30.*

Trace Genealogies

We want the Latter-day Saints from this time to trace their genealogies as far as they can, and to be sealed to their fathers and mothers. Have children sealed to their parents, and run this chain through as far as you can get it. . . .

Brethren and sisters, lay these things to heart. Let us go on with our records, fill them up righteously before the Lord, and carry out this principle, and the blessings of God will attend us, and those who are redeemed will bless us in days to come. I pray God that as a people our eyes may be opened to see, our ears to hear, and our hearts to understand the great and mighty work that rests upon our shoulders, and that the God of heaven requires at our hands.

Millennial Star, *28 May 1894, 338–39, 341.*

Dreams and Visions

I was in Tennessee in the year 1835. . . . I was all by myself and the room was dark; and while I rejoiced in this letter and the promise made to me, I became wrapped in vision. I was like Paul; I did not know whether I was in the body or out of the body. A personage appeared to me and showed me the great scenes that should take place in the last days. One scene after another passed before me. I saw the sun darkened; I saw the moon become as blood; I saw the stars fall from heaven; I saw seven golden lamps set in the heavens, representing the various dispensations of God to man—a sign that would appear before the coming of Christ. I saw the resurrection of the dead. In the first resurrection those that came forth from their graves seemed to be all dressed alike, but in the second resurrection they were as diverse in their dress as this congregation is before me to-day, and if I had been an artist I could have painted the whole scene as it was impressed upon my mind, more indelibly fixed than anything I had ever seen with the natural eye. What does this mean? It was a testimony of the resurrection of the dead. I had a testimony. I believe in the resurrection of the dead, and I know it is a true principle. . . . But what I wanted to say in regard to these matters is, that the Lord does communicate some things of importance to the children of men by means of visions and dreams as well as by the records of divine truth. And what is it all for? It is to teach us a principle. We may never see anything take place exactly as we see it in a dream or a vision, yet it is intended to teach us a principle. My dream gave me a strong testimony of the resurrection. I am satisfied, always have been, in regard to the resurrection. I rejoice in it. The way was opened unto us by the blood of the Son of God.

Deseret News, *25 January 1882.*

Jesus Christ Offered Salvation

The inhabitants of Judah had an idea that if they could only put to death the Messiah, that that would end his mission and work on the earth. Vain hope of that generation as well as this! When they led Jesus to the cross, the very moment that spirit departed from that sorrowful tabernacle, it held the keys of the kingdom of God in all of its strength and power and glory the same as he had done while in the body. And while the body lay in the tomb, Jesus of Nazareth went and preached to the spirits in prison, and when his mission was ended there, his spirit returned again to his tabernacle. Did the Jews kill the principles he taught? No. He burst the bonds of death, he conquered the tomb, and came forth with an immortal body filled with glory and eternal life, holding all the powers and keys he held while in the flesh. Having appeared to some of the holy women and the Apostles, he then went and administered to the Nephites upon this continent, and from here he went to the ten tribes of Israel, and delivered to them the Gospel, and when they return they will bring the history of the dealings of Jesus of Nazareth with them, while in his immortal body. The same unpopularity followed the twelve Apostles. Some of them were sawn asunder, others were beheaded, crucified, etc. But did the Jews destroy the principles they taught? Did they destroy the keys of the kingdom of God? No, verily no. They had no power over these things any more than they had power over the throne of God, or God Himself.

23 October 1881, Journal of Discourses, *22:343.*

Christ Jesus Is the Pattern

Those that live godly in Christ Jesus must suffer persecution. I believe myself, from the reading of the revelations of God, that it is necessary for a people who are destined to inherit the celestial kingdom to be a tried people. I have never read of the people of God in any dispensation passing through life, as the sectarian world would say, on flowery beds of ease, without opposition of any kind. I have always looked upon the life of our Savior—who descended beneath all things that He might rise above all things—as an example for His followers. And yet it has always, in one sense of the word, seemed strange to me that the Son of God, the First Begotten in the eternal worlds of the Father, and the Only Begotten in the flesh, should have to descend to the earth and pass through what He did—born in a stable, cradled in a manger, persecuted, afflicted, scorned, a hiss and bye-word to almost all the world, and especially to the inhabitants of Jerusalem and Judea. There was apparently nothing that the Savior could do that was acceptable in the eyes of the world; anything and almost everything he did was imputed to an unholy influence . . . and so all his life through, to the day of his death upon the cross. There is something about all this that appears sorrowful; but it seemed necessary for the Savior to descend below all things that he might ascend above all things.

Do we comprehend that if we abide the laws of the Priesthood we shall become heirs of God and joint-heirs with Jesus Christ? . . . There was no part of the Gospel that Christ did not fulfill, and he called upon Joseph Smith to fulfill the same. This he did. He laid down his life. He went to the spirit world, and he is there watching over this people. He has power there, and so have our brethren who have gone to the other side of the veil. They are laboring for us. They are watching to see how we perform the work left to our charge.

10 December 1882, Journal of Discourses, *23:327–28, 330.*

Death of Christ

The Savior came and tabernacled in the flesh, and entered upon the duties of the priesthood at 30 years of age. After laboring three and a half years he was crucified and put to death in fulfillment of certain predictions concerning him. He laid down his life as a sacrifice for sin, to redeem the world. When men are called upon to repent of their sins, the call has reference to their own individual sins, not to Adam's transgressions. What is called the original sin was atoned for through the death of Christ irrespective of any action on the part of man; also man's individual sin was atoned for by the same sacrifice, but on condition of his obedience to the Gospel plan of salvation when proclaimed in his hearing.

Millennial Star *(1889), 659.*

Be One

"If ye are not one ye are not mine." The subject that I have upon my mind is, union among the Latter-day Saints. The Savior said to his apostles anciently, and to the apostles in our day: "I say unto you, be one; and if ye are not one ye are not mine." "I and my Father are one." With all the divisions, and all the discontent, and the quarrelings and opposition among the powers on earth, or that have been revealed from heaven, I have never heard that it has ever been revealed to the children of men that there was any division between God the Father, God the Son, and God the Holy Ghost. They are one. They always have been one. They always will be one, from eternity unto eternity. Our Heavenly Father stands at the head, being the Author of the salvation of the children of men, having created and peopled the world and given laws to the inhabitants of the earth. This principle is shown unto us by the revelation of the laws which belong to the different kingdoms. There is a celestial kingdom, a terrestrial kingdom, and a telestial kingdom. There is a glory of the sun, a glory of the moon, and a glory of the stars; and as one star differs from another star in glory, so also is the resurrection of the dead. In the celestial kingdom of God there is oneness—there is union.

Millennial Star *52 (1890), 577.*

Revelations from the Lord

I wish to impress this truth upon the rising generation and all who read this testimony, that the Lord does not give revelations or send angels to men or work miracles to accommodate the notions of any man who is seeking for a sign. When we have the principles of the gospel revealed to us through the mouth of the Savior, or by inspired prophets or apostles, we have no need to ask the Lord to reveal that unto us again.

The Children's Friend, *8:172.*

Faithful and Humble

When any priest, elder, prophet, apostle, or messenger is sent of God to preach the gospel, gather the Saints, work in temples or perform any work for the Lord, and that man is faithful and humble before the Lord in his prayers and duty, and there is any snare or evil in his path, or the righteous to be sought out, or danger to the emigration of the Saints either by sea or land, or knowledge needed in a temple, then the Lord will reveal to him all that is necessary to meet the emergency.

Leaves from My Journal, *4th ed. (Salt Lake City:* Deseret News, *1909), 93–95.*

The Holy Priesthood

The Lord never had a church on the face of the earth, from its first organization until today, unless that church was organized by revelation, with prophets and apostles, pastors, teachers, helps and governments endowed with the Holy Priesthood—that power delegated from God to man, which authorizes him to act for God; and without this Priesthood no man, from the day the world rolled into existence, has any right to administer in any of the ordinances of his holy house, neither has any man a right to that Priesthood save he be called of God.

Deseret News Semi-Weekly, *30 July 1878.*

The Hand of the Lord

We ought to be thankful to the Lord for His mercies unto us. I feel as though His hand has been visible in the establishing of His Church here in the Rocky Mountains, from our first arrival as Pioneers in the valleys of the mountains, when we found a barren desert, until the present. The hand of the Lord has been with this people and with the Elders of Israel, and will continue to be. The Lord is in earnest, in fulfillment of His promises from the creation of the world down to this day with regard to His dispensations to man. I hope and trust that while we dwell in the flesh we all may realize and understand this. It is a great

"The hand of the Lord has been with this people and with the Elders of Israel, and will continue to be. The Lord is in earnest, in fulfillment of His promises from the creation of the world down to this day with regard to His dispensations to man. I hope and trust that while we dwell in the flesh we all may realize and understand this."

In Conference Report, October 1897, 1–2.

blessing to receive the Gospel of Christ, to receive the Holy Priesthood, and to be called to labor in the Priesthood for the salvation of the children of men. This labor is upon us and will remain upon us until the coming of the Son of Man in the clouds of heaven, to reward every man according to the deeds done in the body.

In Conference Report, October 1897, 1–2.

The Great Exemplar

Are we not the sons and daughters of God, and when he shall appear, if we are faithful, shall we not be like him? Yes; and when the glorious day arrives we shall once more have the privilege of standing upon this earth and meeting in joy and thanksgiving . . . thousands of others who have washed their robes white in the blood of the Lamb, and who, through the merits of his atonement, are anointed kings and priests unto God, and with him reign exalted in his kingdom. May we all be found worthy of this reward, and now, while we travel through this world of change and sorrow, may we take pattern by the lives of the worthy . . . and, above all, follow in the steps of the great Exemplar of all righteousness, our Lord Jesus Christ, whose grace be ever with you all.

Millennial Star, *9 July 1888, 436–7.*

5

LORENZO SNOW

Fifth President of
The Church of Jesus Christ
of Latter-day Saints

Born
3 April 1814

Ordained an Apostle
12 February 1849

Years as President
1898–1901

Died
10 October 1901, age 87

God and Man

As man now is, God once was: as God now is, man may be.

The Teachings of Lorenzo Snow, *ed. Clyde J. Williams (Salt Lake City: Bookcraft, 1984), 1.*

I Know God Lives

There is no man that knows the truth of this work more than I do. I know it fully; I know it distinctly. I know there is a God just as well as any man knows it, because God has revealed Himself to me. I know it positively. I shall never forget the manifestations of the Lord; I never will forget them as long as memory endures. It is in me.

In Conference Report, October 1897, 32.

By the Holy Ghost

We testify to the whole world that we know, by divine revelation, even through the manifestations of the Holy Ghost, that Jesus is the Christ, the Son of the living God, and that he revealed himself to Joseph Smith as personally as he did to his apostles anciently, after he arose from the tomb, and that he made known unto him heavenly truths by which alone mankind can be saved.

Deseret News Semi-Weekly, *23 January 1877.*

Knowledge from the Almighty

I testify before this assembly, as I have testified before the people throughout the different States of the Union, and throughout England, Ireland, Scotland, Wales, Italy, Switzerland, and France, that God Almighty, through my obedience to the gospel of Jesus, has revealed to me, tangibly, that this is the work of God, that this is His gospel, that this is His kingdom which Daniel prophesied should be set up in the last days. I prophesy that any man who will be humble before the Lord, any man who will, with childlike simplicity, be baptized for the remission of his sins, shall receive the gift of the Holy Ghost, which shall lead him into all truth and show him things to come; he shall receive a knowledge from the Almighty that His kingdom has been established in these latter days, and that it shall never be thrown down or be left to another people.

Deseret News Weekly, *24 January 1872.*

Gaining a Testimony

My testimony was revealed from heaven. Having become convinced by reasoning, and by listening to the testimony of others who had received these principles, I became satisfied that it was my duty to experiment upon these principles, that I might be able to test the results. This I consequently did, and there followed the same testimony and the same experiences, so far as the knowledge of the divinity of these principles was concerned, as followed obedience to this Gospel as proclaimed by the Apostles in former times. And this knowledge could not be disputed. It was not only acknowledged intellectually, but the inspiration of the Holy Ghost imparted to me a knowledge as physically and as demonstrative as that physical ordinance when I was immersed in the waters of baptism; . . . as I had passed through the atmosphere into the element of water, so my experience, knowledge, and testimony was full and complete, so complete, indeed, that from that day till the present moment, through all of the vicissitudes of life through which I have passed, I have no more doubted the truth of these principles than I do now that I behold this audience, and I never can doubt it. As long as memory continues and reason shall assert its throne, I never can permit the powerful testimony and knowledge that was communicated to me to remain silent. It was revealed to me. The heavens were opened over my head, and the power of God and the light of the Holy Ghost descended and elevated my whole being, and gave me the most perfect knowledge that Jesus was the Son of God. It was not the result simply of opinion or belief, as is the case in many other things, but it was a knowledge far beyond that of belief or opinion. I knew that God had sent His angels and restored the fulness of the Gospel as taught in ancient times; that He sent angels to authorize Joseph Smith, and gave him authority to administer in the ordinances of the Gospel, and to promise the Holy Ghost to all who would be obedient.

Millennial Star, *18 April 1887, 242.*

Help Somebody

When you find yourselves a little gloomy, look around you and find somebody that is in a worse plight than yourself; go to him and find out what the trouble is, then try to remove it with the wisdom which the Lord bestows upon you; and the first thing you know, your gloom is gone, you feel light, the Spirit of the Lord is upon you, and everything seems illuminated.

In Conference Report, April 1899, 2–3.

For the Salvation of the World

When Jesus lay in the manger, a helpless infant, He knew not that He was the Son of God, and that formerly He created the earth. When the edict of Herod was issued, He knew nothing of it; He had not power to save Himself; and His father and mother had to take Him and fly into Egypt to preserve Him from the effects of that edict. Well, He grew up to manhood, and during His progress it was revealed unto Him who He was, and for what purpose He was in the world. The glory and power He possessed before He came into the world was made known unto Him. It was not a very pleasurable thing to be placed upon the cross and to suffer the excruciating torture that He bore for hours, in order to accomplish the work for which He had come upon the earth. It has not been with the Latter-day Saints the most delightful thing that could be imagined to suffer as they have suffered—and what for? For the same as Jesus suffered, to a certain extent—for the salvation of the world.

In Conference Report, April 1901, 3.

He Did Not Fail

Jesus, the Son of God, was sent into the world to make it possible for you and me to receive these extraordinary blessings. He had to make a great sacrifice. It required all the power that He had and all the faith that He could summon for Him to accomplish that which the Father required of Him. . . . He did not fail, though the trial was so severe that He sweat great drops of blood. . . . His feelings must have been inexpressible. He tells us Himself, as you will find recorded in section 19 of the Book of Doctrine and Covenants, that His suffering was so great that it caused even Him "to tremble because of pain, and to bleed at every pore, and to suffer both body and spirit: and would that He might not drink the bitter cup, and shrink." But He had in His heart continually to say, "Father, not my will, but Thine be done."

Millennial Star, *24 August 1899, 531.*

"We testify to the whole world that we know, by divine revelation, even through the manifestations of the Holy Ghost, that Jesus is the Christ, the Son of the living God, and that he revealed himself to Joseph Smith as personally as he did to his apostles anciently, after he arose from the tomb, and that he made known unto him heavenly truths by which alone mankind can be saved."

Deseret News Semi-Weekly, 23 January 1877.

Jesus Honored the Father

Jesus, while travelling here on earth, fulfilling his mission, told the people he did not perform the miracles he wrought in their midst by his own power, nor by his own wisdom; but he was there in order to accomplish the will of his Father. He came not to seek the glory of men, and the honor of men; but to seek the honor and glory of his Father that sent him.

Deseret News, *8 December 1869.*

Divine Manifestations to Lorenzo Snow
(related by his son Le Roi C. Snow)

In 1836, when Lorenzo Snow was twenty-two years of age, and two weeks before he joined the Church, he says: "It was at my sister's [Eliza R. Snow's] invitation that I attended a patriarchal blessing meeting conducted by Father Smith, in the Kirtland temple. I listened with astonishment to him telling the brethren and sisters their parentage, their lineage, and other things which I could not help but believe he knew nothing about, save as the Spirit manifested them unto him." . . .

Six months later Lorenzo Snow, himself, received a patriarchal blessing from Father Smith. Among many other miraculous statements and promises were these: "Thou hast a great work to perform. Thou shalt become a mighty man. There shall not be a mightier man on the earth than thou. Thou shalt have long life; the vigor of thy mind shall not be abated and the vigor of thy body shall be preserved. Thou shalt have power to stand in the flesh and see Jesus."

For some time President Woodruff's health had been failing. Nearly every evening President Lorenzo Snow visited him at his home on South 5th East Street. This particular evening the doctors said President Woodruff was failing rapidly and they feared he would not live much longer.

Lorenzo Snow was then President of the Council of the Twelve and was greatly worried over the possibility of succeeding President Woodruff, especially because of the terrible financial condition of the Church. Referring to this condition President Heber J. Grant has said: "The Church was in a financial slough of despond, so to speak, almost financially bankrupt—its credit was hardly good for a thousand dollars without security."

My father went to his room in the Salt Lake Temple where he was residing at the time. He dressed in his robes of the Priesthood, went into the Holy of Holies, there in the House of the Lord and knelt at the sacred altar. He plead with the Lord to spare President Woodruff's life, that President Woodruff might outlive him and that the great responsibility of Church leadership would never fall upon his shoulders. Yet he promised the Lord that he would devotedly perform any duty required at his hands. At this time he was in his eighty-sixth year.

Soon after this President Woodruff was taken to California where he died Friday morning at 6:40 o'clock September 2nd, 1898. President George Q. Cannon at once wired the sad information to the President's office in Salt Lake City. Word was forwarded to President Snow who was in Brigham City. The telegram was delivered to him on the street in Brigham. He read it to President Rudger Clawson, then president of Box Elder Stake, who was with him, went to the telegraph office and replied that he would leave on the train about 5:30 that evening. He reached Salt Lake City about 7:15, proceeded to the President's office, gave some instructions and then went to his private room in the Salt Lake Temple.

President Snow put on his holy temple robes, repaired again to the same sacred altar, offered up the signs of the Priesthood and poured out his heart to the Lord. He reminded the Lord how he had plead for President Woodruff's life and that his days might be lengthened beyond his own; that he might never be called upon to bear the heavy burdens and responsibilities of Church leadership. "Nevertheless," he said, "Thy will be done. I have not sought this responsibility but if it be Thy will, I now present myself before Thee for Thy guidance and instruction. I ask that Thou show me what Thou wouldst have me do."

After finishing his prayer, he expected a reply, some special manifestation from the Lord. So he waited—and waited—and waited. There was no reply, no voice, no visitation, no manifestation. He left the altar and the room in great disappointment. He passed through the Celestial room and out into the large corridor leading to his own room where a most glorious manifestation was given President Snow. One of the most beautiful accounts of this experience is told by his granddaughter, Allie Young Pond.

"One evening when I was visiting Grandpa Snow in his room in the Salt Lake Temple, I remained until the doorkeepers had gone and the night-watchman had not yet come in, so grandpa said he would take me to the main, front entrance and let me out that way. He got his bunch of keys from his dresser.

"After we left his room and while we were still in the large corridor, leading into the celestial room, I was walking several steps ahead of grandpa when he stopped me saying: 'Wait a moment Allie, I want to tell you something.

"'*It was right here that the Lord Jesus Christ appeared to me at the time of the death of President Woodruff. He instructed me to go right ahead and reorganize the First Presidency of the Church at once and not wait as had been done after the death of the previous presidents, and that I was to succeed President Woodruff.*'

"Then grandpa came a step nearer and held out his left hand and said 'He stood right here, about three feet above the floor. It looked as though He stood on a plate of solid gold.'

"Grandpa told me what a glorious personage the Savior is and described His hands, feet, countenance and beautiful, white robes, all of which were of such a glory of whiteness and brightness that he could hardly gaze upon Him.

"Then grandpa came another step nearer me and put his right hand on my head and said: 'Now, granddaughter, I want you to remember that this is the testimony of your grandfather, that he told you with his own lips that he actually saw the Savior here in the Temple, and talked with Him face to face.'

"Then we went on and grandpa let me out of the main, front door of the Temple."

During the M.I.A. June conference in 1919 at the officers' testimony meeting in the Assembly Hall I [Le Roi Snow] related Allie Young Pond's experience and testimony. President Heber J. Grant immediately arose and said:

"In confirmation of the testimony given by Brother LeRoi C. Snow quoting the granddaughter of Lorenzo Snow, I want to call attention to the fact that several years elapsed after the death of the Prophet Joseph Smith before President Young was sustained as the president of the Church; after the death of President Young, several years elapsed again before President Taylor was sustained, and again when he died several years elapsed before President Woodruff was sustained.

"After the funeral of President Wilford Woodruff the Apostles met in the office of the First Presidency and Brother Francis M. Lyman said: 'I feel impressed although one of the younger members of the quorum, to say that I believe it would be pleasing in the sight of the Lord if the First Presidency of the Church was reorganized right here and right now. If I am in error regarding this impression, President Snow and the senior members of the council can correct me.'

"President Snow said that he would be pleased to hear from all the brethren upon this question, and each and all of us expressed ourselves as believing it would be pleasing to the Lord and that it would be the proper thing to have the Presidency organized at once.

"When we had finished, then and not till then, did Brother Snow tell us that he was instructed of the Lord in the Temple the night after President Woodruff died, to organize the Presidency of the Church at once."

Tuesday, September 13, 1898, eleven days after President Woodruff's death and five days after his funeral the Council of the Apostles met at 10 o'clock A.M. in the President's Office.

Lorenzo Snow was thus sustained by the Council of the Apostles, as President of the Church of Jesus Christ of Latter-day Saints. . . .

Sun, Sept. 18, 1898, five days after he was sustained by the Council of the Apostles as president of the Church, Pres. Snow said in the Salt Lake Tabernacle:

"I can assure you, brethren and sisters, that I had no ambition to assume the responsibility which now rests upon me. If I could have escaped it honorably I should never have been found in my present position, but the Lord revealed to me that this was His will."

Le Roi C. Snow, Deseret News/Church Department, *2 April 1938, 3, 8.*

Revelation

We should try to learn the nature of [the spirit of revelation]. . . . This is the grand means that the Lord has provided for us, that we may know the light, and not be groveling continually in the dark.

In Conference Report, April 1899, 52.

Pay Tithing

It is the word of the Lord to you, my brethren and sisters, that you should conform to that which is required of you as a people who have these glorious prospects of exaltation and glory before you. What is it? Why, it is something that has been drummed into your ears from time to time until you perhaps have got tired of hearing it. . . . The word of the Lord to you is not anything new; it is simply this: THE TIME HAS NOW COME FOR EVERY LATTER-DAY SAINT, WHO CALCULATES TO BE PREPARED FOR THE FUTURE AND TO HOLD HIS FEET STRONG UPON A PROPER FOUNDATION, TO DO THE WILL OF THE LORD AND TO PAY HIS TITHING IN FULL. That is the word of the Lord to you, and it will be the word of the Lord to every settlement throughout the land of Zion. After I leave you and you get to thinking about this, you will see yourselves that the time has come when every man should stand up and pay his tithing in full. The Lord has blessed us and has had mercy upon us in the past; but there are times coming when the Lord requires us to stand up and do that which He has commanded and not leave it any longer. What I say to you in this Stake of Zion I will say to every Stake of Zion that has been organized. There is no man or woman that now hears what I am saying who will feel satisfied if he or she fails to pay a full tithing.

Deseret Evening News, *18 May 1899.*

Manifestations

There is no man that knows the truth of this work more than I do. I know it fully; I know it distinctly. I know there is a God just as well as any man knows it, because God has revealed Himself to me. I know it positively. I shall never forget the manifestations of the Lord; I never will forget them as long as memory endures. It is in me.

In Conference Report, Oct. 1897, 32.

6

JOSEPH F. SMITH

Sixth President of The Church of Jesus Christ of Latter-day Saints

Born
13 November 1838

Ordained an Apostle
1 July 1866

Years as President
1901–1918

Died
19 November 1918, age 80

Deep in My Heart

I desire to bear my testimony to you; for I have received an assurance which has taken possession of my whole being. It has sunk deep into my heart; it fills every fiber of my soul; so that I feel to say before this people, and would be pleased to have the privilege of saying it before the whole world, that God has revealed unto me that Jesus is the Christ, the Son of the living God, the Redeemer of the world.

Gospel Doctrine, *5th ed. (Salt Lake City: Deseret Book Company, 1939), 501.*

Our Beacon

I have absolute confidence in [Jesus Christ]. My whole heart and soul goes out with love for Him. My hopes are built upon His glorious character and His word. He was without sin; He was spotless, and possessed power unto life eternal; He opened the way from the grave to everlasting life for me and all the children of men. My confidence in Him is boundless. My love for Him surpasses all else on earth, when I possess the Spirit of the Gospel as I should, and He to me is first and foremost. He is the greatest of all that has ever sojourned in this world of ours, and He came to be our beacon light, our guide and exemplar, and it is our business to follow Him.

In Brian H. Stuy, comp., Collected Discourses Delivered by President Wilford Woodruff, His Two Counselors, the Twelve Apostles, and Others, *5 vols. (1987–92), 5:55–56.*

The Power of the Son of God

It is by the power of God that all things are made that have been made. It is by the power of Christ that all things are governed and kept in place that are governed and kept in place in the universe. It is the power which proceeds from the presence of the Son of God throughout all the works of his hands, that giveth light, energy, understanding, knowledge, and a degree of intelligence to all the children of men, strictly in accordance with the words in the Book of Job, "There is a spirit in man; and the inspiration of the Almighty giveth them understanding."

Improvement Era, *1907–8, 380.*

A Fulness

Even Christ himself was not perfect at first; he received not a fulness at first, but he received grace for grace, and he continued to receive more and more until he received a fulness. Is not this to be so with the children of men? Is any man perfect? Has any man received a fulness at once? Have we reached a point wherein we may receive the fulness of God, of his glory and his intelligence? No; and yet if Jesus, the Son of God, and the Father of the heavens and the earth in which we dwell, received not a fulness at the first, but increased in faith, knowledge, understanding and grace until he received a fulness, is it not possible for all men that are born of women to receive little by little, line upon line, precept upon precept, until they shall receive a fulness, as he has received a fulness, and be exalted with him in the presence of the Father?

Improvement Era, *1907–8, 380.*

The Lord Speaks to Man's Immortal Soul

Whenever the Lord speaks to man, he speaks to his immortal soul, and satisfaction and unsurpassing peace and joy come to all who listen. Happy is the man, indeed, who can receive this soul-satisfying testimony, and be at rest, and seek for no other road to peace than by the doctrines of Jesus Christ. His perfected philosophy teaches also that it is better to suffer wrong than to do wrong, and to pray for our enemies and for those who despitefully use us. . . . No other philosopher has ever said as Jesus said, "Come unto me."

Improvement Era, *1903–4, 717.*

Who Would Welcome Christ's Rule?

I believe in God's law. I believe that it is his right to rule in the world. I believe that no man has or should have any valid objection in his mind to the government of God, and the rule of Jesus Christ, in the earth. Let us suppose, for a moment, that Christ were here and that he was bearing rule in the world. Who would come under his condemnation? Who would be subject to his chastening word? Who would be in disharmony or unfellowship with God? Would the righteous man? Would the virtuous man? the pure and virtuous woman? the pure and honest in heart? the upright? the straightforward? those who do the will of heaven? Would they be in rebellion to Christ's rule if He were to come here to rule? No. They would welcome the rule and reign of Jesus Christ in the earth. They would welcome His law and acknowledge His sovereignty, they would hasten to rally to His standard and to uphold the purpose and the perfection of His laws and of His righteousness. Who would, then, be recreant to the rule of Christ? The whoremonger, the adulterer, the liar, the sorcerer, he who bears false witness against his neighbor, he who seeks to take advantage of his brother and who would overcome and destroy him for his own worldly gain or profit; the murderer, the despiser of that which is good, the unbeliever in the eternities that lie before us, the atheist, perhaps, although I think that he would not be so far from Christ as some that profess to be teachers of His doctrines and advocates of His laws. . . . Such as these would be the people who would not welcome the reign of Jesus Christ. Are there any who profess to be Latter-day Saints in this class, and would fear to have Christ reign and rule?

In Conference Report, April 1904, 4.

Wealth of His Inner Soul

In our day, there is a tendency to count men of little value who are not rich in worldly means and influence; who can not on this day bestow presents upon family and friends, and extend such acts of charity as find their way to the newspapers. But Christ, the ideal, the model, declared of himself: "The foxes have holes, and the birds of the air have nests; but the Son of man hath not where to lay his head." Yet now he is of all value, and exercises all influence, for only through him are we saved. But it was not the influence of wealth, nor the lavish gifts of gold that made him rich and gave him power. It was the spirit of his Father, the wealth of his inner soul.

Who that can not build a great house, or control vast interests, in our day, is looked upon by those who can, as of only small consequence and little use among men; but with all his poverty, Christ was rich in help, for when the tempest arose, and his disciples came to him in their anguish, calling, "Lord, save us; we perish," he arose and rebuked the wind and the sea, and there was a great calm, causing the men to marvel at his power, that even the winds and the sea obey him!

Improvement Era, *1904–5, 146.*

The Witness of the Spirit of God

I want to bear my testimony to you Latter-day Saints. I know that my Redeemer lives. We have all the testimony and all the evidence of this great and glorious truth, that the world has, that is, all that the so-called Christian world possesses; and, in addition to all that they have, we have the testimony of the inhabitants of this western continent, to whom the Savior appeared, and delivered His gospel, the same as He delivered it to the Jews. In addition to all this new testimony and the testimony of the holy scriptures from the Jews, we have the testimony of the modern Prophet, Joseph Smith, who saw the Father and the Son, and who has borne record of them to the world; whose testimony was sealed with his blood, and is in force upon the world today. We have the testimony of others who witnessed the presence of the Son of God, in the Kirtland temple, when He appeared to them there, and the testimony of Joseph and Sidney Rigdon, who declared that they were the last witnesses of Jesus Christ. Therefore, I say again, I know that my Redeemer lives; for in the mouths of these witnesses this truth has been established in my mind.

Beside these testimonies, I have received the witness of the Spirit of God in my own heart, which exceeds all other evidences, for it bears record to me, to my very soul, of the existence of my Redeemer, Jesus Christ. I know that He lives, and that in the last day He shall stand upon the earth, and that He shall come to the people who shall be prepared for Him, as a bride is prepared for the bridegroom, when He shall come.

In Conference Report, October 1910, 4.

The Savior of Mankind

Christ is indeed the Savior of my soul, the Savior of mankind. He has sacrificed his life for us that we might be saved, he has broken the bands of death, and has bid defiance to the grave, and bids us follow him. He has come forth from death unto life again, he has declared himself to be the way of salvation, the light and the life of the world, and I believe it with all my heart. I not only believe it, but as I know that the sun shines so I know that belief in him inspires to good and not to evil; and as I know that his spirit prompts to purity of life, to honor, to uprightness, to honesty and to righteousness, and not to evil, so I know by all the proofs that it is possible for me to grasp that Jesus is the Christ, the Son of the living God, the Savior of mankind.

Yet with all this, with this assurance in my heart, with this knowledge that I have received, if I stop here, what good will it do me? Of what good will this knowledge be to me? What will this knowledge alone avail? It will avail this, that having received that testimony in my heart, having received in my soul the witness of the spirit of the living god, that Jesus is the Christ, and I stop there and go not any further, that very witness in my soul will add to my eternal damnation. Why? Because it is not only our duty to know that Jesus is the Christ but to keep the influence of his spirit in our souls. It is not only necessary to have his testimony in our hearts, but it is necessary that we should do the things that he has commanded, and the works of righteousness that he did, in order that we may attain to the exaltation that is in store for his children who do as well as believe.

Improvement Era, *1906, 806–8.*

A Sure Foundation

From my boyhood I have desired to learn the principles of the gospel in such a way and to such an extent that it would matter not to me who might fall from the truth, who might make a mistake, who might fail to continue to follow the example of the Master, my foundation would be sure and certain in the truths that I have learned though all men else go astray and fail of obedience to them. We all have heard of people who have pinned their faith to the arm of flesh, who have felt that their belief, their confidence and their love for the principles of the gospel of Jesus Christ would be shattered if their ideals—those possibly who first taught them the principles of the Gospel—should make a mistake, falter or fall.

I know of but one in all the world who can be taken as the first and only perfect standard for us to follow, and He is the Only Begotten Son of God.

"I desire to bear my testimony to you; for I have received an assurance which has taken possession of my whole being. It has sunk deep into my heart; it fills every fiber of my soul; so that I feel to say before this people, and would be pleased to have the privilege of saying it before the whole world, that God has revealed unto me that Jesus is the Christ, the Son of the living God, the Redeemer of the world."

Gospel Doctrine, 501.

I would feel sorry, indeed, if I had a friend or an associate in this life who would turn away from the plan of life and salvation because I might stumble or make a failure of my life. I want no man to lean upon me nor to follow me, only so far as I am a consistent follower in the footsteps of the Master.

Juvenile Instructor, *1915–16, 738–39.*

Honor the Doctrine

I do not believe in the ideas that we hear sometimes advanced in the world, that it matters but little what men do in this time, if they will but confess Christ at the end of their journey in life, that that is all-sufficient, and that by so doing they will receive their passport into heaven. I denounce this doctrine. It is unscriptural, it is unreasonable, it is untrue, and it will not avail any man, no matter by whom this idea may be advocated; it will prove an utter failure unto men. As reasonable beings, as men and women of intelligence, we cannot help but admire and honor the doctrine of Jesus Christ, which is the doctrine of God, and which requires of every man and woman righteousness in their lives, purity in their thoughts, uprightness in their daily walk and conversation, devotion to the Lord, love of truth, love of their fellow-man, and above all things in the world the love of God. These were the precepts that were inculcated by the Son of God when He walked among His brethren in the meridian of time. He taught these precepts; He exemplified them in His life, and advocated continually the *doing* of the will of Him that sent Him.

In Conference Report, October 1907, 3.

Witnesses in the Bible

I read the Bible in which I find narrations of many of his doings, says, precepts, and examples. And I do not believe that any upright, honest man or woman, possessing common intelligence, can read the gospels of the New Testament and testimonies therein given of the Savior, without intuitively feeling that he was what he professed to be. For every upright, honest person is possessed, more or less, of the Holy Spirit, and this holy messenger in the hearts of men bears record of the word of God; and when all such read these inspired writings, with honesty of heart and meekness of spirit, divested of prejudices and the false conceptions arising from traditions and erroneous training, the Spirit of the Lord bears witness in unmistakable language that burns with conviction, therefore, I believe that Jesus was the Christ, the Savior, the only begotten of the Father.

Deseret News Semi-Weekly, *30 April 1878.*

At Rest in Christ

What does it mean to enter into the rest of the Lord? Speaking for myself, it means that through the love of God I have been won over to Him, so that I can feel at rest in Christ, that I may no more be disturbed by every wind of doctrine, by the cunning and craftiness of men, whereby they lie in wait to deceive; and that I am established in the knowledge and testimony of Jesus Christ, so that no power can turn me aside from the straight and narrow path that leads back into the presence of God, to enjoy exaltation in His glorious kingdom; that from this time henceforth I shall enjoy that rest until I shall rest with Him in the heavens.

Millennial Star, *30 May 1907.*

Vision of the Redemption of the Dead

The eyes of my understanding were opened, and the Spirit of the Lord rested upon me, and I saw the hosts of the dead, both small and great. And there were gathered together in one place an innumerable company of the spirits of the just, who had been faithful in the testimony of Jesus while they lived in mortality; and who had offered sacrifice in the similitude of the great sacrifice of the Son of God, and had suffered tribulation in their Redeemer's name. All these had departed the mortal life, firm in the hope of a glorious resurrection, through the grace of God the Father and his Only Begotten Son, Jesus Christ. . . .

While this vast multitude waited and conversed, rejoicing in the hour of their deliverance from the chains of death, the Son of God appeared, declaring liberty to the captives who had been faithful; and there he preached to them the everlasting gospel, the doctrine of the resurrection and the redemption of mankind from the fall, and from individual sins on conditions of repentance. But unto the wicked he did not go, and among the ungodly and the unrepentant who had defiled themselves while in the flesh, his voice was not raised; neither did the rebellious who rejected the testimonies and the warnings of the ancient prophets behold his presence, nor look upon his face.

Where these were, darkness reigned, but among the righteous there was peace; and the saints rejoiced in their redemption, and bowed the knee and acknowledged the Son of God as their Redeemer and Deliverer from death and the chains of hell. Their countenances shone, and the radiance from the presence of the Lord rested upon them, and they sang praises unto his holy name.

I marveled, for I understood that the Savior spent about three years in his ministry among the Jews and those of the house of Israel, endeavoring to teach them the everlasting gospel and call them unto repentance; and yet, notwithstanding his mighty works, and miracles, and proclamation of the truth, in great power and authority, there were but few who hearkened to his voice, and rejoiced in his presence, and received salvation at his hands. But his ministry among those who were dead was limited to the brief time intervening between the crucifixion and his resurrection; and I wondered at the words of Peter—wherein he said that the Son of God preached unto the spirits in prison, who sometime were disobedient, when once the long-suffering of God waited in the days of Noah—and how it was possible for him to preach to those spirits and perform the necessary labor among them in so short a time.

And as I wondered, my eyes were opened, and my understanding quickened, and I perceived that the Lord went not in person among the wicked and the disobedient who had rejected the truth, to teach them; but behold, from among the righteous, he organized his forces and appointed messengers, clothed with power and authority, and commissioned them to go forth and carry the light of the gospel to them that were in darkness, even to all the spirits of men; and thus was the gospel preached to the dead. . . .

Thus was it made known that our Redeemer spent his time during his sojourn in the world of spirits, instructing and preparing the faithful spirits of the prophets who had testified of him in the flesh; that they might carry the message of redemption unto all the dead, unto whom he could not go personally, because of their rebellion and transgression, that they through the ministration of his servants might also hear his words. . . .

I beheld that the faithful elders of this dispensation, when they depart from mortal life, continue their labors in the preaching of the gospel of repentance and redemption, through the sacrifice of the Only Begotten Son of God, among those who are in darkness and under the bondage of sin in the great world of the spirits of the dead. . . .

Thus was the vision of the redemption of the dead revealed to me, and I bear record, and I know that this record is true, through the blessing of our Lord and Savior, Jesus Christ, even so. Amen.

Doctrine and Covenants 138:11–14, 18–30, 36–37, 57, 60.

I Bear Testimony

I know that my Redeemer lives. I feel it in every fiber of my being. I am just as satisfied of it as I am of my own existence. I cannot feel more sure of my own being than I do that my Redeemer lives, and that my God lives, the Father of my Savior. I feel it in my soul; I am converted to it in my whole being. I bear testimony to you that this is the doctrine of Christ, the gospel of Jesus, which is the power of God unto salvation.

Improvement Era, *1908, 386.*

"Christ is indeed the Savior of my soul, the Savior of mankind. He has sacrificed his life for us that we might be saved, he has broken the bands of death, and has bid defiance to the grave, and bids us follow him."

Improvement Era, 1906, 806–8.

If I Am Faithful

I want to say as a servant of God, independent of the testimonies of all men and of every book that has been written, that I have received the witness of the Spirit in my own heart, and I testify before God, angels and men, without fear of the consequences that I know that my Redeemer lives, and I shall see Him face to face, and stand with Him in my resurrected body upon this earth, if I am faithful; for God has revealed this unto me. I have received the witness, and I bear my testimony, and my testimony is true.

Gospel Doctrine, 447.

HEBER J. GRANT

Seventh President of The Church of Jesus Christ of Latter-day Saints

Born
22 November 1856

Ordained an Apostle
16 October 1882

Years as President
1918–1945

Died
14 May 1945, age 88

Truly the Savior of the World

To members of the Church throughout the world, and to peace-lovers everywhere, we say, behold in this Man of Galilee not merely a great Teacher, not merely a peerless Leader, but the Prince of Peace, the Author of Salvation, here and now, literally and truly the Savior of the World!

In Messages of the First Presidency, 6:39.

Know God

The birth of Christ our lord was more than an incident, it was an epoch in the history of the world to which prophets had looked forward, of which poets had sung, and in which angels joined their voices with mortals in praise to God. It was the day decreed and foreordained by our Father who is in heaven when he would manifest himself to his children, who are here upon earth, in the person of his Only Begotten Son.

He came that man might see and know God as he is, for

he bore witness that whoever had seen him had seen the Father, for he was the express image of his person.

In Messages of the First Presidency, *5:246.*

What Joseph Smith Saw

I rejoice that the Church of Jesus Christ is founded upon the first great vision that was enjoyed by the boy Joseph Smith over one hundred years ago. He declare that he saw two heavenly Beings, whose glory and grandeur were beyond the power of man to describe and that one of them addressed him and pointed to the other and said: "This is my beloved Son, hear Him." [See Joseph Smith—History 1:17.] There cannot be any doubt in the heart of a Latter-day Saint regarding Jesus Christ's being the Son of the living God, because God Himself introduced Him to Joseph Smith.

Gospel Standards, *comp. G. Homer Durham (Salt Lake City: Deseret Book Company, 1941), 23–24.*

Keep the Commandments

We are told that faith without works is dead; that as the body without the spirit is dead, so also is faith without works dead, and I am sorry to say that there are many professed Latter-day Saints who are spiritually dead. We many times ask ourselves the question, why does this man progress in the plan of life and salvation, while his neighbor, of equal intelligence and ability, of apparently the same testimony and power, and perchance greater power, stands still? I will tell you why. One keeps the commandments of our Heavenly Father, and the other fails to keep them. The Savior says that he that keeps his commandments is the man that loves him, and he that keeps the commandments of God shall be loved of the Father, and the Savior says he will love him and he will manifest himself unto him. The Lord also tells us that those who hear His sayings and doeth them shall be likened unto the wise man who built his house upon the rock, and when the rains descended and the floods came and the winds blew and beat upon that house, it fell not, because it was founded upon a rock. . . .

I have met many young men who have said to me, "I do not know that the Gospel is true. I believe it, but I do not know it." I have invariably replied to them that our Lord and Master has said that he who will do the will of the Father shall know of the doctrine, whether it be of God, or whether he spoke of himself, and if they would do the will of the Father, they should eventually have a knowledge of the Gospel. Some of them have said: "Oh, if I could only see an angel; if I could only hear speaking in tongues; if I could only see some great manifestation, then I would believe." I wish to say to all within the sound of my voice that the seeing of angels and great manifestations do not make great men in the Church and kingdom of God. Think of the three witnesses to the Book of Mormon. What is their testimony? It is that an angel showed them the plates, and that they knew they had been translated by the gift and power of God. How did they claim to know this? Because "His voice hath declared it unto us . . . an angel of God came down from heaven . . . we beheld and saw the plates, and the engravings thereon . . . the Lord commanded us that we should bear record of it." Yet these men fell by the wayside, though they remained true and steadfast to their testimony of the Book of Mormon. . . .

Think of it, beholding the glory of the Son and receiving a fullness of that glory, and hearing the voice declare that he is the only Begotten of the Father, and yet this man, Sidney Rigdon, proved a traitor to the Prophet and fell by the wayside! . . .

So it has been in all ages of the world, and so it will be with those who do not keep the commandments of God. Angels may visit them, they may see visions, they may have dreams, they may even see the Son of God, and yet the Spirit of God will not burn in their hearts. But those who do the will of God, and live God-like lives, they will grow and increase in the testimony of the Gospel and in power and ability to do God's will.

In Conference Report, April 1900, 21–23.

Testifying Brings Joy

To me, one of the greatest testimonies of the divinity of the mission of our Savior is the joy and happiness that we all experience whenever we testify that He was in very deed the Son of God and the Redeemer of the world. I know of nothing that brings greater joy, except testifying regarding the divinity of the mission of the Savior, than to testify regarding the divinity of the mission of the Prophet Joseph Smith.

There is but one path of safety to the Latter-day Saints, and that is the path of duty. It is not a testimony, it is not marvelous manifestations, it is not knowing that the Gospel of Jesus Christ is true, that it is the plan of salvation, it is not actually knowing that the Savior is the Redeemer, and that Joseph Smith was His prophet, that will save you and me, but it is the keeping of the commandments of God, the living the life of a Latter-day Saint.

I have been profoundly impressed upon many occasions, as I have studied the history of the early men in this church, with the fact that one-half of the first quorum of Apostles fell by the wayside; that all of the three witnesses to the Book of Mormon, who saw the angel, who heard the voice of God, who heard the Lord testify to them that this work had been translated by the gift and power of God, that the Lord Himself, by His voice from heaven, had told these men to bear witness of this fact—should also fall by the wayside. The same with a majority of the eight witnesses. Oliver Cowdery, who heard the Savior's voice, and beheld a heavenly messenger before the Church was organized, gave a description, which is recorded in the Pearl of Great Price, of his ordination, in connection with the Prophet, to the Aaronic Priesthood, stating it was beyond the language of man to paint the joy and the grandeur that surrounded them upon that occasion. He also had the Apostles of the Lord Jesus Christ, who lived upon the earth in the days of our Savior, lay their hands upon his head and ordain him to the Melchizedek, or the Higher Priesthood. In the Kirtland Temple, with the Prophet Joseph Smith, he saw the Savior, also Moses, Elias, and Elijah. He had given to him, in connection with the Prophet, every key and every authority of all the dispensations of the Gospel of Jesus Christ, from the earliest time down to the present, and yet by failing to do his duty, by failing to keep the commandments of God, this man lost his standing in the Church of Christ. True, he repented and came back. The same is true of Martin Harris. . . .

There is not a Latter-day Saint living who is keeping the commandments of the Lord, who would not regard it as one of the greatest joys imaginable if he could testify that he had heard the voice of God, and that the Lord had given him a commandment; and that, in fulfillment of the requirement of the Lord, he had recorded in this testimony: "we bear witness of these things." How we all would rejoice to be able to bear such a testimony; provided we had the Spirit of God; provided we were so living that it was not a dead letter with us.

In Conference Report, April 1915, 82–83.

Power of Christ

When I was a young unmarried man, another young man who had received a doctor's degree ridiculed me for believing in the Book of Mormon. [A] . . . statement that this doctor made was this: that the voice of man can only carry a few hundred feet, and yet the Book of Mormon teaches that when Jesus Christ was resurrected and came to this country he spoke to the people and his voice was heard all over the land, not alone by the people that were near, but all over the land. "That is a lie," said he, "and you know it." I said, "That is no lie at all. Jesus Christ, under God, was the Creator of this earth, and if he had the power and ability to create the earth I believe that he could arrange for his voice to carry all over the world at one and the same time."

In Conference Report, April 1929, 129–30.

The Divinity of the Work

God help you and me and every Latter-day Saint to prove to the Lord by our lives, that our testimony of the divinity of this work is not merely lip service. . . . God bless every man that believes in Jesus Christ and is working for the uplift of mankind, and God defeat every man who ridicules the Savior of the world, the Redeemer of mankind.

In Conference Report, October 1934, 132.

The Father of Christ

When we say that we believe in God we mean that we believe in him as an individuality, as actually the Father of Jesus Christ—not a congeries of laws floating through the universe without form and void, but we believe him to be the Father of Jesus Christ. He is the God whom we as Latter-day Saints worship; and we believe Jesus Christ to be, not only one of the great moral teachers, the greatest the world has ever known, but the Son of God, the Redeemer of mankind, that he came to earth with a divinely appointed mission, to die on the cross, in order that you and I and all eventually may have part in the resurrection.

In Conference Report, April 1935, 10.

God and Jesus Christ Did Come

I have met hundreds of men who have said, "If it were not for Joseph Smith I could accept your religion." Any man who does not believe in Joseph Smith as a prophet of the true and the living God has no right to be in this Church. That revelation to Joseph Smith is the foundation stone. If Joseph Smith did

"To members of the Church throughout the world, and to peace-lovers everywhere, we say, behold in this Man of Galilee not merely a great Teacher, not merely a peerless Leader, but the Prince of Peace, the Author of Salvation, here and now, literally and truly the Savior of the World!"

In *Messages of the First Presidency,* 6:39.

not have that interview with God and Jesus Christ the whole Mormon fabric is a failure and a fraud. It is not worth anything on earth. But God did come, God did introduce his Son, God did inspire that man to organize the Church of Jesus Christ, and all the opposition of the world is not able to withstand the truth. It is flourishing, it is growing, and it will grow more.

In Conference Report, October 1939, 128.

Jesus Is the Christ

I bear witness to you, although I have not seen the Savior sitting upon the right hand of God, I know that He lives; that I know that Jesus is the Christ; that I know that Joseph Smith was a prophet of God; I know that the signs follow the believer; I know that hands are laid upon the sick and that the sick do recover; I know that we have the gift of tongues among the Latter-day Saints; I know that we have visions, dreams, and revelations.

In Conference Report, April 1899, 28–29.

We Believe in God

A gentleman sent out several hundred letters to representative ministers, and asked them the question: "Do you believe in God, a personal God, a definite and tangible intelligence, not a congeries of laws floating like a fog in the universe, but God a person, in whose image you were made?" Not a minister answered, "yes." They said they could not be certain about a thing of that kind. . . .

We declare to all the world that God lives, that He is the Father of our spirits, that He is absolutely the Father of Jesus Christ, that Jesus Christ is the Redeemer of the world. Men say we lack liberality and breadth, because we say we are the only true Church. We are not lacking in liberality or breadth; the

Redeemer of the world, Jesus Christ, our Lord and Savior, said it, and we are repeating what He said.

In Conference Report, April 1922, 11–12.

The Lord Makes No Mistakes

It has never ceased to be a wonder to me that I do represent the Lord here upon the earth. My association from childhood with the remarkable and wonderful men that have preceded me has made it almost overwhelming to think of being in the same class with them.

The last words uttered by President Joseph F. Smith were to the effect, when he shook hands with me—he died that night—"The Lord bless you, my boy, the Lord bless you; you have got a great responsibility. Always remember this is the Lord's work and not man's. The Lord is greater than any man. He knows whom He wants to lead His Church, and never makes any mistake. The Lord bless you."

I have felt my own lack of ability. In fact when I was called as one of the Apostles I arose to my feet to say it was beyond anything I was worthy of, and as I was rising the thought came to me, "You know as you know that you live that John Taylor is a prophet of God, and to decline this office when he had received a revelation is equivalent to repudiating the Prophet." I said, "I will accept the office and do my best." I remember that it was with difficulty that I took my seat without fainting.

There are two spirits striving with us always, one telling us to continue our labor for good, and one telling us that with the faults and failings of our nature we are unworthy. I can truthfully say that from October 1882, until February 1883, that spirit followed me day and night telling me that I was unworthy to be an Apostle of the Church, and that I ought to resign. When I would testify of my knowledge that Jesus is the Christ, the Son of the Living God, the

Redeemer of mankind, it seemed as though a voice would say to me: "You lie! You lie! You have never seen Him."

While on the Navajo Indian reservation with Brigham Young, Jr., and a number of others, six or eight, on horse back, and several others in "white tops"—riding along with Lot Smith at the rear of that procession, suddenly the road veered to the left almost straight, but there was a well beaten path leading ahead. I said: "Stop, Lot, stop. Where does this trail lead? There are plenty of foot marks and plenty of horses' hoof marks here." He said, "It leads to an immense gully just a short distance ahead, that is impossible to cross with a wagon. We have made a regular 'Muleshoe' of miles here to get on the other side of the gully."

I had visited the day before the spot where a Navajo Indian had asked George A. Smith, Jr., to let him look at his pistol. George A. handed it to him, and the Navajo shot him.

I said, "Lot, is there any danger from Indians?"

"None at all."

"I want to be all alone. Go ahead and follow the crowd." I first asked him if I allowed the animal I was riding to walk if I would reach the road on the other side of the gully before the horsemen and the wagons, and he said, "Yes."

As I was riding along to meet them on the other side I seemed to see, and I seemed to hear, what to me is one of the most real things in all my life, I seemed to see a Council in Heaven. I seemed to hear the words that were spoken. I listened to the discussion with a great deal of interest. The First Presidency and the Council of the Twelve Apostles had not been able to agree on two men to fill the vacancies in the Quorum of the Twelve. There had been a vacancy of one for two years, a vacancy of two for one year, and the Conference had adjourned without the vacancies being filled. In this Council the Savior was present, my father was there, and the Prophet Joseph Smith was there. They discussed the question that a mistake had been made in not filling those two vacancies and that in all probability it would be another six months before the Quorum would be completed, and they discussed as to whom they wanted to occupy those positions, and decided that the way to remedy the mistake that had been made in not filling these vacancies was to send a revelation. It was given to me that the Prophet Joseph Smith and my father mentioned me and requested that I be called to that position. I sat there and wept for joy. It was given to me that I had done nothing to entitle me to that exalted position, except that I had lived a clean, sweet life. It was given to me that because of my father having practically sacrificed his life in what was known as the great Reformation, so to speak, of the people in early days, having been practically a martyr, that the Prophet Joseph and my father desired me to have that position, and it was because of their faithful labors that I was called, and not because of anything I had done of myself or any great thing that I had accomplished. It was also given to me that that was all these men, the Prophet and my father, could do for me; from that day it depended upon me and upon me alone as to whether I made a success of my life or a failure. . . .

I have been happy during the twenty-two years that it has fallen my lot to stand at the head of this Church. I have felt the inspiration of the Living God directing me in my labors. . . . I have known as I know that I live, that I am entitled to the light and the inspiration and the guidance of God in directing His work here upon this earth; and I know, as I know that I live, that it is God's work, and that Jesus Christ is the Son of the Living God, the Redeemer of the world and that He came to this earth with a divine mission to die upon the cross as the Redeemer of mankind, atoning for the sins of the world.

In Conference Report, April 1941, 4–6.

Greater the Joy

It is a remarkable fact that we can never read of the labors which [Jesus Christ] performed, or listen to others speaking of the great work which he accomplished,

"I bear witness to you, although I have not seen the Savior sitting upon the right hand of God, I know that He lives; that I know that Jesus is the Christ; that I know that Joseph Smith was a prophet of God."

In Conference Report, April 1899, 28–29.

without taking pleasure in it, while on the other hand, there is nothing so interesting in the life and history of any other individual but what by hearing and reading it time and time again we become tired of it. I can bear testimony, from my own experience, that the oftener I read of the life and labors of our Lord and Savior Jesus Christ the greater are the joy, the peace, the happiness, the satisfaction that fill my soul in contemplating what he did.

In Conference Report, April 1944, 7.

A Witness

I leave with you my testimony that God lives, that Jesus is the Christ, that Joseph Smith was and is a prophet of God. How do I know it? I know it as well as I know that I live. I know heat; I know cold; I know joy, and I know sorrow; and say to you that in the hour of sorrow, in the hour of affliction, in the hour of death, God has heard and answered my prayers, and I know that He lives. I leave my testimony with you.

In Conference Report, October 1944, 13.

Simon Dewey

GEORGE ALBERT SMITH

Eighth President of The Church of Jesus Christ of Latter-day Saints

Born
4 April 1870

Ordained an Apostle
8 October 1903

Years as President
1945–1951

Died
4 April 1951, age 81

His Companionship

I have been buoyed up and, as it were, lifted out of myself and given power not my own to teach the glorious truths proclaimed by the Redeemer of the world. I have not seen Him face to face but have enjoyed the companionship of His spirit and felt His presence in a way not to be mistaken. I know that my Redeemer lives and gladly yield my humble efforts to establish His teachings. . . . Every fibre of my being vibrates with the knowledge that He lives and some day all men will know it.

Forace Green, comp., Testimonies of Our Leaders *(Salt Lake City: Bookcraft, 1958), 53.*

Jesus Christ, Our Savior

I rejoice this day in a testimony of the divinity of the mission of Jesus Christ, the Redeemer of the world. I know, as I know that I live, that He is what we believe Him to be.

I know that there is no other name under heaven whereby we may hope to gain exaltation, but the name of Jesus Christ, our Savior.

In Conference Report, April 1916, 48.

No Other Name in Heaven

Above all, I thank him for the knowledge that has been burned into my soul; I know that my heavenly Father lives, I know that Jesus Christ is the Savior of mankind, and that there is no other name under heaven whereby men and women may be exalted, but the name of Jesus Christ, our Lord. I do know that he came into the world in this latter day, that he bestowed divine authority upon a humble boy who was seeking the truth, and the result of that has been the organization of the Church with which we are identified; and there is with it the power of God unto salvation to all those who believe.

In Conference Report, October 1927, 50.

He Labored in Love and Kindness

When our Savior in humility came upon earth, the people said, "Who are you, that you should claim to be the Son of God? We know your father; he is Joseph, the carpenter. We know your mother; she is Mary. We have Moses and Abraham for our prophets, and we have no need of a man like you to come and speak to us in the name of the Lord." He went among them and ministered to the sick, healed the afflicted, unstopped the ears of the deaf, restored the blind to sight, cleansed the leper by His magic touch, raised the dead to life. Then they said He performed these wondrous works by the power of Beelzebub. Yet He was indeed the Son of God. He labored among them in love and kindness; but they cast His name out as evil. They even cast reproach upon the city from which He came, and said, "Can any good thing come out of Nazareth?" . . .

The same feeling that was entertained, to some extent, against the Savior has continued in the earth. People who do not understand the things of God because they have not the Spirit of God, reviled and cast them out as evil, when in fact the evil is in themselves. . . .

Our Heavenly Father . . . chose and commissioned Joseph Smith, as He had done other prophets, to go forth among the people and speak in the name of the Lord. Through this humble instrument, the Gospel was restored to the earth again and he preached the same doctrines that our Savior taught while He was upon the earth. Under the Lord's direction, he organized the Church of Christ, with apostles, prophets, pastors, teachers, evangelists, etc., as the Church should be organized, to continue thus until all should come to a unity of the faith. He ministered unto the people, he healed the sick; he loved the souls of the children of men. But, as had been the case with prophets whom the Lord had raised up before, it seemed necessary in this case that the testimony of His servant should be sealed with his life's blood. . . . You remember when he was first raised up how the people of this country said, "We have no need of you. You are Joseph, the son of Joseph, and we know where you come from. You are not a strong and mighty man, and you do not come from an influential family. We have no need of new revelation. We have the Bible, and that is all that is necessary for the salvation of the children of men." . . . The people of the world, as before, judge this work by the spirit of man. They do not have the Spirit of God, which would enable them to understand that it came from our Father in heaven.

In Conference Report, April 1904, 63–64.

At the Right Hand

I have found many in the world who have not known that we believe in the divine mission of our Lord, and I have been led to say upon more than one occasion that there are no people in the world who so well understand the divine mission of Jesus Christ, who so thoroughly believe him to have been the Son of

God, who are so sanguine [certain] that at the present time he is enthroned in glory at the right hand of his Father, as the Latter-day Saints.

Deseret News, *27 December 1924, Church section.*

Your School Master

You have had the greatest instructor that the world knows anything about. You have had for your school master the King of kings, the Lord of lords, the Creator of the heavens and the earth; who in his wonderful tenderness and consideration for us in this day, has sent his prophet into the world to explain to us, and to make clear to our minds the things that he gave to the world hundreds of years ago that have been misunderstood and have been misinterpreted very much to the detriment of our Father's children. But in our day he has renewed to us the truth, has given to us the blessed teachings that should qualify us to be men and women after his own heart, has held out to us the promise that if we will do the things that he advises our lives will be pure and holy, peace will be our portion here, and we shall dwell with him throughout the ages of eternity. What more could he give unto us, or, . . . "What more can he say than to you he has said, you who unto Jesus for refuge have fled?"

In Conference Report, October 1923, 73.

Repent

The Redeemer of mankind was more than a good man who came into the world to teach us ethics. The Redeemer of mankind possessed more than ordinary intelligence. He is indeed the Son of God, the only begotten in the flesh. . . . He came to call men to repentance, to turn them from the error of their way. He went among them representing God the Eternal Father, proclaiming that he was in the image of his Father, and that those who had seen him had seen the Father, and told them that he had been sent to do the will of his Father, and called on all men to turn from error that had crept in among them, to repent of their sins and go down into the water of baptism.

In Conference Report, October 1921, 39.

To Be Taught by the Lord

How grateful we ought to be that there has been removed from us the doubt that exists in the minds of so many of our Father's splendid sons and daughters, that there has come to us that abiding assurance that God lives, that Jesus is the Christ, that he is our elder brother, and that if we are faithful, in his own due time he will cleanse and purify this earth on which we dwell, and it will be celestialized, and those who have prepared themselves for the celestial kingdom will have the joy of dwelling hereon, to be directed, to be counseled, to be taught, and advised by the Lord of lords and King of kings, throughout the ages of eternity. What a wonderful promise . . . has been given to the children of men, and oh, how I pray that there may come into the souls of the thousands and millions of God's children a knowledge of the purpose of their being, that they may prepare, while there is yet time before their final summons, for the time when we will be classified and placed in whatever kingdom we have earned the right to dwell in, when we go to the other side.

In Conference Report, October 1925, 33–34.

The Church of Jesus Christ

We have the peculiar distinction of belonging to a Church that does not have the name of any man, because it was not organized by the wisdom of any man. It was named by the Father of us all in honor of his Beloved Son, Jesus Christ.

I would like to suggest to you . . . that we honor the name of the Church. It is not the church of James and John, it is not the church of Moroni, nor is it the church of Mormon. It is the Church of Jesus Christ. And while all these men were wonderful and notable characters, we have been directed to worship God in a church that bears the name of his Beloved Son. . . .

When Christ came to instruct the people, he told them that there must be faith in God and righteousness in life or they would not please our Heavenly Father. And so the Savior of the world came with kindness and love. He went among the people healing the sick, unstopping the ears of the deaf, and restoring sight to those who were blind. They saw these things done by the power of God. Comparatively few of them could understand or believe that he was the Son of God.

In Conference Report, October 1945, 167–69.

He Spoke for His Father

He was the Son of God, and He did have the right to speak in the name of the Father. The truths He brought to the earth came from the Father; and though they nailed Him to the cross, though they placed upon His head the plaited crown of thorns, and put the mock scepter in His hands, though they spilled His blood with the cruel spear, yet the words that He delivered to them was the word of the Lord, and He was indeed the Son of God.

In Conference Report, April 1904, 63.

Crucify Him

In the time of the Savior the adversary whispered to [the] people, he is not the Son of God, surely you will not accept him, he is just an ordinary man, he is only the son of Mary and Joseph and he is not any more the Son of God than you are, and the people listened to that insidious, wicked one and crucified the Redeemer of mankind.

In Conference Report, April 1918, 39.

"I rejoice this day in a testimony of the divinity of the mission of Jesus Christ, the Redeemer of the world. I know, as I know that I live, that He is what we believe Him to be. I know that there is no other name under heaven whereby we may hope to gain exaltation, but the name of Jesus Christ, our Savior."

In Conference Report, April 1916, 48.

Cruelly Tortured

His only Begotten Son in the flesh had to call the attention of his associates to the fact that with all his majesty and his royalty, he still must live like other men. And when the time came for him to die, and be hung upon the cross, and cruelly tortured by those of his own people, his own race, he did not become angry, he did not resent the unkindness.

When the one thief on the cross railed against him, the other thief called attention to the fact that they were only receiving their just desserts, while here was a righteous man being unjustly punished. The one thief prayed, as best he knew how to pray, and the Savior of the World said to this man who was suspended alongside him on another cross:

" . . . To day shalt thou be with me in paradise." (Luke 23:43.)

The people of the world do not understand some of these things, and particularly, many men cannot understand how the Savior felt when in the agony of his soul, he cried to his Heavenly Father, not to condemn and destroy these who were taking his mortal life, but he said:

" . . . Father, forgive them; for they know not what they do." (Luke 23:34.)

That should be the attitude of all the members of The Church of Jesus Christ of Latter-day Saints. That should be the attitude of all the sons and daughters of God and would be, it seems to me, if they fully understood the plan of salvation. . . . So it is our privilege, possessing divine authority that has been conferred again in our day, to go into the world and teach men the message of the Savior that would have redeemed the world if people had accepted it.

In Conference Report, October 1945, 167–69.

Other Sheep

What more direct evidence of resurrection from the dead could have been had than that he, in his resurrected body, came among [the Nephites] and taught them the same Gospel that he taught in Jerusalem? And he now fulfilled the promise he had made in Jerusalem when he said, "Other sheep I have which are not of this fold; them also I must bring and they shall hear my voice; and there shall be one fold and one shepherd." [John 10:16.] He came in his resurrected body to bring to them the information he had predicted should be given to those to whom he now ministered.

It was a wonderful experience for those people. After teaching them all day . . . he healed their sick and blessed their children and continued to instruct them in the beauty of his Gospel. There was no doubt in their minds that he was the Savior of the world. They saw him come from heaven and witnessed his marvelous power. . . . He came in glory. Angels came down from heaven as it were in the midst of fire and surrounded the little children so that they were encircled with fire. And the angels did minister unto them.

Those were not hallucinations, but experiences of such marvelous character as to be remembered forever by those who experienced them. As Latter-day Saints we accept this record as evidence of the resurrection of Jesus Christ our Lord.

In Conference Report, April 1939, 121–22.

Some Are Just Here

This poor old world today would not be in the condition it is in if the people who live on it believed in God, the Eternal Father, and in His Son, Jesus Christ, and in the Holy Ghost. People talk about believing, but two-thirds of those who live on this earth know practically nothing at all about the God of Abraham, Isaac and Jacob. Of the other one-third, the so-called Christians, about fifty per cent know very little about the personality of God, and know very little about being here for any particular reason; they are just here. . . . .

I know that God lives, I know that Jesus is the Christ, I know that Joseph Smith was and is a prophet of the living God, that the Gospel of our Lord is here on earth and we have the opportunity to conform our lives to its principles and be blessed thereby.

I realize that there are some who say, "I can't believe," but that does not change my knowledge of the truth. I know it just the same. I know another thing, that if I were not telling the truth in testifying as I do, I would have to account to my Heavenly Father for seeking to deceive. I am taking into account what it all means. I realize the seriousness of my testimony and here in the presence of all of you I leave that witness.

28 April 1946 address at graduation exercises, Wasatch LDS Seminary, Heber City, Utah, LDS Church Archives.

Seriousness of Testimony

We are not out of the woods. This world is in for a housecleaning unless the sons and daughters of our Heavenly Father repent of their sins and turn to him. And that means the Latter-day Saints, or members of the Church of Jesus Christ of Latter-day Saints, along with all the rest, but we, first of all, ought to be setting the example. . . . I know that God lives. I know that Jesus is the Christ. I know that Joseph Smith was a Prophet of the Living God, and had restored to him the true gospel of Jesus Christ in these latter days.

That might sound like boasting if it were not so serious. It is serious, and I know that I will have to answer for that testimony as I leave it with you. . . . It will not be long until this man who is talking will have finished his work and passed to the other side, and when I go, I want to be worthy to join my grandparents and my parents, my brothers and sisters who have passed on. I know they have earned a place that is worth while. I want to go where they have gone, and I know that if I were not to tell you the truth in regard to this matter, I might lose that opportunity.

So, realizing the seriousness of a testimony like that, realizing what it means, and with love unfeigned and a desire to be a blessing to all our Father's children, I leave this witness with you that this is the gospel of Jesus Christ, the only power of God unto salvation in preparation for the celestial kingdom, into which kingdom we may all go if we will, but it will be on his terms.

In Conference Report, October 1946, 153.

Part of the Lord's Work

We are thankful to him who is the Author of our being, and grateful that he came down to earth and brought with him his Beloved Son to begin a new dispensation—the Dispensation of the Fullness of Times. This is not the Church of Joseph Smith or of any other leader who followed him. This is the Church of Jesus Christ, and it was our Heavenly Father who gave it its name.

I wonder sometimes if we realize what an honor it is to have membership in this great organization. Even in our business affairs and in our social affairs we should carry with us the feeling, "I am a part of the work of the Lord, and I desire to be worthy of the blessings that have come to me." . . .

Some people have worshiped the sun; some have worshiped other luminaries; and some have worshiped mountains and other things, with the thought that it was worship. But the worship in the Church of Jesus Christ of Latter-day Saints is a devoted life, a desire to be worthy of him in whose image we have been created and who has given us all that the world has that is worth while—the gospel of Jesus Christ.

In Conference Report, April 1949, 7–8.

Righteous Living

Joseph was a prophet who gave his life for the cause. Hyrum was a patriarch who gave his life, and many others have given their lives also for the gospel of Jesus Christ. This is the Lord's work; His authority is deposited with this Church, and nowhere else in all the world except with the Church. Knowing that, I am happy to be here with you. I am delighted to be able to worship with

"I know that Jesus Christ is the Savior of mankind, and that there is no other name under heaven whereby men and women may be exalted, but the name of Jesus Christ, our Lord."

In Conference Report, October 1927, 50.

you in this house that is sacred to us all. I pray that when we go from here, each of us will return to our homes with a renewed determination that we will be worthy of him who gives us all our blessings, that we will be worthy of one another as we live together in our homes, sanctified by the righteousness of our lives.

In Conference Report, April 1947, 167.

Simon Dewey

9

DAVID O. McKAY

Ninth President of
The Church of Jesus Christ
of Latter-day Saints

Born
8 September 1873

Ordained an Apostle
9 April 1906

Years as President
1951–1970

Died
18 January 1970, age 96

Healing in His Wings

The rising sun can dispel the darkness of night, but it cannot banish the blackness of malice, hatred, bigotry, and selfishness from the hearts of humanity. Happiness and peace will come to earth only as the light of love and human compassion enter the souls of men.

It was for this purpose that Christ, the Son of righteousness, "with healing in his wings," came in the Meridian of Time. Through him wickedness shall be overcome, hatred, enmity, strife, poverty, and war abolished. . . .

Men may yearn for peace, cry for peace, and work for peace, but there will be no peace until they follow the path pointed out by the Living Christ.

Improvement Era, *1964, 1041–42.*

Peace and Good Cheer

Jesus said in his Sermon on the Mount: "Blessed are the peacemakers: for they shall be called the children of God." (Matt. 5:9.) . . . Toward the closing scenes of his mortal life, he said to his disciples: "These things I have spoken unto you, that in me ye might have peace. In the world ye shall have tribulation: but be of good cheer; I have overcome the world." (John 16:33.)

On the same occasion he said: "Peace I leave with you, . . . not as the world giveth, give I unto you. Let not your heart be troubled, neither let it be afraid." (John 14:27.)

All through his life peace was on his lips and in his heart, and when he came forth from the tomb and appeared unto his disciples, his first greeting was "Peace be unto you." (John 20:19.)

Peace as taught by the Savior is exemption from individual troubles, from family quarrels, from national difficulties. Such peace refers to the person just as much as it does to the community. That man is not at peace who is untrue to the whisperings of Christ, the promptings of his conscience. He cannot be at peace when he is untrue to his better self, when he transgresses the law of righteousness, either in dealing with himself, in indulging in passion or appetites, in yielding to the temptations of the flesh, in being untrue to trust, or in transgressing the law of righteousness in dealing with his fellowmen.

Improvement Era, *March 1968, 2–3.*

Other Gods

Too many men and women have other gods to which they give more thought than to the resurrected Lord—the god of pleasure, the god of wealth, the god of indulgence, the god of political power, the god of popularity, the god of race superiority—as varied and numerous as were the gods of ancient Athens and Rome. . . .

It is therefore a blessing to the world that there are occasions . . . which, as warning semaphores, say to mankind: *In your mad rush for pleasure, wealth, and fame, pause and think what is of most value in life.*

No man can sincerely resolve to apply to his daily life the teachings of Jesus of Nazareth without sensing a change in his own nature. The phrase, "born again," has a deeper significance than many people attach to it. This *changed feeling* may be indescribable, *but it is real.* Happy [is] the person who has truly sensed the uplifting, transforming power that comes from this nearness to the Savior, this kinship to the Living Christ.

Improvement Era, *1962, 404–5.*

Apply Christ's Teachings

The Church of Jesus Christ of Latter-day Saints believes that in his life and teachings Jesus Christ reveals a standard of personal living and of social relations that, if fully embodied in individual lives and in human institutions, would not only ameliorate the present ills of society, but would also bring happiness and peace to mankind.

If it be said that . . . so-called Christian nations have failed to achieve such a goal, we answer that all failure to do so may be found in the fact that they have failed to apply the principles and teachings of true Christianity. . . .

. . . The human family has suffered from unrestrained expressions and manifestations of selfishness, hatred, envy, greed—animal passions that have led to war, devastation, pestilence, and death. If even the simplest principles of the Savior's teachings had been observed, history would have been changed.

Improvement Era, *January 1970, 2.*

What You Think of Christ

What you sincerely think in your heart of Christ will determine what you are, will largely determine what your acts will be. No person can study His divine personality, can accept His teachings, or follow His example, without becoming conscious of an uplifting and refining influence within himself.

Juvenile Instructor, *1967, 99.*

Resisting Satan's Temptations

Latter-day Saints are members of the Church . . . for the developing of the religious sentiment, the true religious spirit. This may be done in two ways: first, by *seeking the truth*, and *living in harmony* with it; and second, by *resisting every influence, every power* that *tends to destroy or to dwarf in any way the religious sentiment*. . . .

Take as an example the Savior. After He passed through that ordinance [baptism] to fulfill all righteousness, after He had received the commendation of the Father and the testimony from on high that He was the Son of God, the "Beloved Son" in whom the Father was well pleased, Satan was there ready to thwart His mission. Jesus went forth in fasting and prayer, preparatory for the great mission resting upon Him; and when in His weakest moment—as Satan thought—when His body was weak and exhausted by long fasting, the evil one presented himself in temptation; and what was the temptation? An appeal to His bodily weakness: "If thou be the Son of God—(note the taunt—the very testimony on the bank of the Jordan was, "This is my beloved Son;") "If thou be the Son of God, command that these stones be made bread." In a moment of weakness and hunger, that temptation would be strongest, other things being equal.

There was the moment of *resistance* on Jesus' part. His *seeking* had been manifested in prayer and fasting; His resistance came, at the moment of bodily weakness. Though the body was weak the Spirit was strong and Christ answered: "It is written, man shall not live by bread alone, but by every word that proceedeth out of the mouth of God." Then Satan tried Him on another point. Failing in that, the tempter tried Him still on the third, tempted Him first on His love for physical comfort; second, tempted Him on vanity, and third, tempted Him on love for worldly wealth, and the power to rule the world. But all these temptations Christ resisted; and the final resistance was: "Get thee behind me Satan, for it is written: Thou shalt worship the Lord thy God and Him only shalt thou serve." . . . In some way the evil one will attack us. In some way he can weaken us; in some way he will bring before us that which will weaken our souls, and will tend to thwart that true development of religious sentiment; and what I mean by that is this: the development of the spirit within, the strengthening of the inner man, the strengthening and growth of the spirit, that time cannot kill, but which is enduring and lasting as the eternal Father of that spirit. And the things that will tend to dwarf this spirit or to hinder its growth are things that the Latter-day Saints are called upon to resist.

In Conference Report, April 1907, 11–12.

Always Remember Him

The sacrament is a memorial of Christ's life and death. When we think of his life we think of sacrifice. Not a moment of his existence on earth did Christ think more of himself than he did of his brethren and the people whom he came to save, always losing himself for the good of others, and finally giving his life for the redemption of mankind. When we partake of the sacrament in his presence we remember him, his life of sacrifice, and service; and we are inspired by that thought and memory. There is nothing won in this life without sacrifice.

The partaking of the sacrament indicates also how communion with Christ may be secured. It cannot be obtained by Sunday righteousness and week-day indulgence. It implies that we will remember Christ always.

In Conference Report, October 1929, 11–13.

Washed Their Feet

When the Savior was about to leave his Apostles, he gave them a great example of service. You remember he girded himself with a towel and washed his disciples' feet.

Returning the basin to the side of the door, ungirding himself, and putting on his robe, he returned to his position with the Twelve, and said: "Ye call me Master and Lord: and . . . so I am."

In Conference Report, April 1951, 158–59.

Vision of the City Eternal

I . . . fell asleep, and beheld in vision something infinitely sublime. In the distance I beheld a beautiful white city. Though far away, yet I seemed to realize that trees with luscious fruit, shrubbery with gorgeously tinted leaves, and flowers in perfect bloom abounded everywhere. The clear sky above seemed to reflect these beautiful shades of color. I then saw a great concourse of people approaching the city. Each one wore a white flowing robe and a white headdress. Instantly my attention seemed centered upon their leader, and though I could see only the profile of his features and his body, I recognized him at once as my Savior. The tint and radiance of his countenance were glorious to behold. There was a peace about him which seemed sublime—it was divine!

The city, I understood, was his. It was the City Eternal; and the people following him were to abide there in peace and eternal happiness.

But who were they?

As if the Savior read my thoughts, he answered by pointing to a semicircle that then appeared above them, and on which were written in gold the words:

These Are They Who Have Overcome The World—
Who Have Truly Been Born Again!

Experienced on ship while nearing Samoa, recorded in 10 May 1921 entry in David O. McKay's world tour diary, in Cherished Experiences from the Writings of David O. McKay, *comp. Clare Middlemiss (Salt Lake City: Deseret Book Company, 1976), 59–60.*

The Great High Priest

The Priesthood came direct from our Lord and Savior, Jesus Christ, who is the great High Priest, and he authorized Peter, James and John, on whom he

"What a glorious condition will be in this old world when it can truthfully be said to Christ, the Redeemer of mankind, "All men seek for thee" (Mark 1:37). Selfishness, envy, hatred, lying, stealing, cheating, disobedience, quarreling, and fighting among nations will then be no more."

In Conference Report, April 1968, 9.

bestowed that Priesthood, to bestow it upon the Prophet Joseph Smith; and John the Baptist, who held the Aaronic Priesthood to bestow the Aaronic Priesthood upon Joseph Smith. Joseph Smith did not take it; it came direct, and you brethren . . . can trace your ordination, probably within five steps, right back to the Savior himself.

In Conference Report, October 1955, 91.

The Shepherds Were Prepared

In Micah, the fifth chapter, Bethlehem, the City of David, is mentioned by that prophet as the birthplace of the Messiah. I wonder if the shepherds, to whom the revelation of Christ's birth was given, had not that prophecy in mind as they kept watch over their flocks by night.

A revelation of God does not come to man unless he prepares himself for it and lives worthy of it. Evil influences will thrust themselves upon men, but God will be sought. Evil is always crowding and tempting and promising. God asks us to put forth effort and seek: " . . . Seek, and ye shall find; knock, and it shall be opened unto you." (Matthew 7:7.) But *we* must seek, *we* must knock; and I think the humble shepherds were treasuring in their hearts the hope, as all Judea was treasuring it, that the Messiah would soon come. Those humble men had opened to them the vision of God.

"And it came to pass, as the angels were gone away from them into heaven, the shepherds said one to another, Let us now go even unto Bethlehem, and see this thing which is come to pass, which the Lord hath made known unto us." (Luke 2:15.)

The shepherds did not say, "I wonder if this be true?" They did not say, "Let us go and see if this thing be true." They said, "Let us . . . go . . . and see this thing which is come to pass, which the Lord hath made known unto us"—an assurance that God had revealed His Son; that the angels had given to the world the message that He who would be King of kings, and Lord of lords, had come as a mere babe in the humblest part of that little Judean town. . . .

How can we get that peace of which the angels sang, and which the shepherds found in that little limestone grotto with Mary lying there in a stable; not a stable as we picture it, but a cave in the limestone rock where the animals were kept, near where their keepers slept?

To get that peace is one of the greatest blessings that can come to mortal man. It comes not by lethargy, nor inactivity, but *by doing the Will of God*—that peace which Christ had in mind when after His resurrection He appeared to the Twelve and said " . . . Peace be unto you: . . ." (John 20:21.)

Juvenile Instructor, *1962, 397–98.*

Meditation and Prayer

Meditation is one of the most secret, most sacred doors through which we pass into the presence of the Lord. Jesus set the example for us. As soon as he was baptized and received the Father's approval—"This is my beloved Son, in whom I am well pleased" (Matt. 3:17)—Jesus repaired to what is now known as the Mount of Temptation where, during forty days of fasting, he communed with himself and his Father and contemplated the responsibility of his own great mission. One result of this spiritual communion was such strength as enabled him to say to the tempter: "Get thee hence, Satan: for it is written, Thou shalt worship the Lord thy God, and him only shalt thou serve." (Matt. 4:10.)

Before he gave the beautiful Sermon on the Mount, he was in solitude, in communion. He did the same thing after that busy Sabbath day, when he arose early in the morning after having been the guest of Peter. Peter undoubtedly found the guest chamber empty, and when he and others sought Jesus, they found him alone. It was on that morning that they said: "All men seek for thee." (Mark 1:37.)

Again, after Jesus had fed the 5,000 he told the Twelve to dismiss the multitude. Then Jesus, the historian says, went to the mountain for solitude and "when the evening was come, he was there alone." (Matt. 14:23.) Meditation! Prayer!

Improvement Era, *June 1967, 80.*

Seek Him

What a glorious condition will be in this old world when it can truthfully be said to Christ, the Redeemer of mankind, "All men seek for thee" (Mark 1:37). Selfishness, envy, hatred, lying, stealing, cheating, disobedience, quarreling, and fighting among nations will then be no more.

In Conference Report, April 1968, 9.

Our Comfort and Inspiration

"How can we know the way?" asked Thomas, as he sat with his fellow apostles and their Lord at the table after the supper on the memorable night of the betrayal; and Christ's divine answer was: "I am the way, the truth, and the life. . . ." (John 14:5–6.) And so he is! He is the source of our comfort, the inspiration of our life, the author of our salvation. If we want to know our relationship to God, we go to Jesus Christ. If we would know the truth of the immortality of the soul, we have it exemplified in the Savior's resurrection.

My testimony of the risen Lord is just as real as Thomas', who said to the resurrected Christ when he appeared to his disciples: "My Lord and my God." (John 20:28.) I know that he lives. He is God made manifest in the flesh; and I know that "there is none other name under heaven given among men, whereby we must be saved." (Acts 4:12.)

I know that he will confer with his servants who seek him in humility and in righteousness. I know because I have heard his voice, and I have received his guidance in matters pertaining to his kingdom here on earth.

I know that his Father, our Creator, lives. I know that they appeared to the Prophet Joseph Smith and revealed to him the revelations which we now have recorded in the Doctrine and Covenants and in other Church works. This knowledge is as real to me as that which occurs in our daily lives. When we lay our bodies down at night, we know—we have an assurance—that the sun will rise in the morning and shed its glory over all the earth. So near to me is the knowledge of Christ's existence and divinity of this restored Church.

Improvement Era, *June 1968, 2–3, 5.*

Simon Dewey

JOSEPH FIELDING SMITH

Tenth President of The Church of Jesus Christ of Latter-day Saints

Born
19 July 1876

Ordained an Apostle
7 April 1910

Years as President
1970–1972

Died
2 July 1972, age 95

Redemption through Christ

I know that Jesus Christ is the Redeemer of the world, that he came into the world to take upon him the transgression of every soul who would repent; and that we, through our repentance and our faith and our acceptance of the principles of the gospel, shall receive full salvation through the shedding of his blood and through the atonement which he brought to pass that we might receive these blessings. Moreover, I know that all men shall be redeemed from death, because men are not responsible for death, therefore Jesus Christ has redeemed them from death through the shedding of his blood. They shall rise in the resurrection, every man to receive his reward according to his works. We who have received the truth of the everlasting gospel ought not to be satisfied with anything short of the best, and the best is the fulness of the Father's kingdom; and for that I hope and pray we shall live and set examples in righteousness to all men that none may stumble, that none may falter, that none may turn from the path of righteousness, due to anything that we may do or say.

In Conference Report, April 1923, 139.

Truth about Jesus Christ Shall Endure

If there is any one thing that brings joy and peace and satisfaction to the heart of man, beyond anything else that I know, it is the abiding testimony which I have, and which you have, that Jesus Christ is the Son of God. That is a truth that cannot be changed. Men may attack it; they may ridicule it; they may declare that he is not the Redeemer of the world, that his mission was not true, or that its purpose, through the shedding of his blood, was not to grant unto all men the remission of sins on condition of their repentance. They may refuse to believe in the resurrection from the dead, or even that Christ himself came forth, as the Scriptures declare, after he had been put to death by his enemies; nevertheless the truth remains. He did die for the sins of the world, he did bring to pass redemption from death, he did grant unto men the opportunity of repentance, and remission of sins through their belief and acceptance of the principles of the gospel, and of his mission. These truths are fundamental, they shall endure; they cannot be destroyed no matter what men may say or think.

In Conference Report, October 1924, 100–1.

The Soul of Man

I have a firm testimony of the mission of our Redeemer, and it is my duty, so far as I have the power, to raise my voice and to declare unto the people, not only of the Latter-day Saints, but in all the world, that Jesus is the Christ, the Son of the living God. . . .

I believe, and you believe, all Latter-day Saints believe, in the literal resurrection of the body and its reuniting with the spirit, thus becoming, as the scriptures inform us, the soul of man. The resurrection of the Son of God was typical. We are informed that his body did not see corruption, although it was placed in the tomb and remained there for the three days. . . . That body was taken up and spirit and body again united inseparably, and in that form he appeared unto his disciples who were unconvinced when he appeared to them and "were terrified and affrighted," the scriptures say, thinking they had seen a spirit. He manifested to them that it was himself, and called upon them, in order to convince them that it was the body that was laid in the tomb, to come and handle him and see for themselves that it was his body that had been pierced and they thrust their hands into the wounds in his hands, his feet and his side.

As he arose from the dead, so shall all men rise; both the just and the unjust shall come forth from the grave. The sea shall give up its dead; the grave shall give up its dead; all shall come forth and stand before the judgment seat of God to be judged according to their works. They shall not all come forth at the same time. Those who are Christ's shall come forth at his coming.

In Conference Report, April 1917, 58, 62–63.

Honor the Father through the Son

The Savior taught that no man can testify of God and reject his Son; and that no man can deny that Jesus Christ is the Redeemer of the world and believe in the Father who sent him. We must honor the Father through the Son, and he who rejects the Son and denies the power of the resurrection knows not God. Again the Savior said:

"He that believeth on the Son hath everlasting life, and he that believeth not the Son shall not see life, but the wrath of God abideth on him."

This does not mean that those who reject the Son shall not come forth in the resurrection, for all shall be raised from the dead, but the unbeliever shall not partake of eternal life in the kingdom of God where dwell the Father and the Son. It is, however, the purpose of the Father to extend the power of the resurrection to all men, through the atonement of the Son, and thus give immortality to all his children.

In Conference Report, April 1926, 40–41.

Bread and Water

When the Savior stood at the well in conversation with the woman of Samaria, he gave her some very important instruction regarding eternal life. There he also declared himself to be the Son of God. He asked her for water to drink, and in turn promised her, and all who would believe on him and keep his sayings, that to them he would give water which if they would drink of it they would never thirst. . . .

On another occasion when teaching the Jews, they asked Jesus what sign he could show, or what great work he had accomplished, to prove his ministry. They referred to Moses and to the manna that the Lord had sent to the children of Israel when they were in the wilderness. The Lord answered them thus:

"Verily, verily, I say unto you, Moses gave you not that bread from heaven, but my Father giveth you the true bread from heaven.

"For the bread of God is he that cometh down from heaven, and giveth life unto the world."

So he declared himself to be the water of life and the bread of life, and made the promise that those who would receive this water and this bread should never thirst, and never hunger, their souls would be satisfied. They misunderstood him; the woman thought he spoke of water which quenches thirst. The Jews thought he spoke of bread which sustains the body, but he was speaking of the principles of the gospel, these principles of eternal life which, if the people would live them, would bring them back into the presence of the Father. . . .

Those who do not dwell there shall not know them, for they shall not be blessed with eternal life, which is God's life, although they may be in possession of immortality, for all men will receive the gift of the resurrection through

"If there is any one thing that brings joy and peace and satisfaction to the heart of man, beyond anything else that I know, it is the abiding testimony which I have, and which you have, that Jesus Christ is the Son of God. That is a truth that cannot be changed."

In Conference Report, October 1924, 100–1.

the atonement of Jesus Christ. We must have faith in Jesus Christ as the Son of God. We must believe in the Father, in the Son, and in the Holy Ghost, as three separate and distinct personages, the Father and the Son having bodies of flesh and bones, not blood.

In Conference Report, October 1925, 112, 114–15.

His Witnesses

When the Savior ministered among men, he said: "I am not sent but unto the lost sheep of the house of Israel," and after his resurrection he did not appear to the high priest and the members of the Sanhedrin, and say to them: "I told you I was the Son of God, and that I would rise from the dead, and you did not believe me." He did not appear to Pilate and say to him: "When you asked me if I am the King of the Jews, I said to you, 'Thou sayest' and now you will be convinced for I am risen from the dead." He did not appear to any of his enemies; but he did appear to his disciples and commissioned them and sent them forth to declare to the world that he had risen from the dead. It was Peter, James and John and the other apostles who declared to the Jews, after his resurrection: "We are his witnesses," and they were sent to testify to all the world.

To all who offer their criticisms against Joseph Smith for the manner in which the Book of Mormon came forth, we might say in the same sort of criticism: Why did not our Lord appear to the scribes and rulers of the Jews after his resurrection and convince them that he was in very deed the Son of God? Why did he not go to Pilate and set him right and bring him into his fold? What a wonderful thing this would have been. Then all the enemies would have been convinced and his great work would have spread more rapidly, for all men would have believed. This is, as the story of Lazarus proves, foolish reasoning. That is not the way the Lord performs his great work. From the beginning of time he has always presented his message to the world through chosen witnesses. The course followed by Joseph Smith is consistent. He did that which he was commanded. It was the plan before the foundation of the world that in this mortal life men should walk by faith, not by sight, but withal, aided by the sacred word which the Lord would reveal to his servants the prophets.

13 August 1944 radio address, in The Restoration of All Things *(Salt Lake City: Deseret News Press, 1945), 103–6.*

The Great Suffering

We cannot comprehend the great suffering that the Lord had to take upon himself to bring to pass this redemption from death and from sin. He spent a few years upon the earth, and during that short sojourn he suffered the abuse of men. They stoned him; they spat upon him; they cursed him; they ridiculed him; they accused him of almost every crime they could think of, and finally they took him and crucified him upon a cross.

We get into the habit of thinking, I suppose, that his great suffering was when he was nailed to the cross by his hands and his feet and was left there to suffer until he died. As excruciating as that pain was, that was not the greatest suffering that he had to undergo, for in some way which I cannot understand, but which I accept on faith, and which you must accept on faith, he carried on his back the burden of the sins of the whole world. It is hard enough for me to carry my own sins. How is it with you? And yet he had to carry the sins of the whole world, as our Savior and the Redeemer of a fallen world, and so great was his suffering before he ever went to the cross, we are informed, that blood oozed from the pores of his body, and he prayed to his Father that the cup might pass if it were possible, but not being possible he was willing to drink.

In Conference Report, October 1947, 147–48.

The First Vision

For some fifteen hundred years or more, perhaps, the world had lost the truth in relation to the Father and the Son. . . . In the year 325, at a conclave that was held, they adopted a new idea entirely in regard to God and confused the Father and the Son, and the Christian world, from that day down until now, has looked upon the Father and the Son as being mysterious—I cannot say individuals, nor can I say substance, but some sort of spirit without separation[.] And the idea of the separate individuals, Father and Son, from that day on ceased to exist.

Now, if the Prophet was telling a falsehood when he went into the woods to pray, he never would have come out and said that he had seen a vision of the Father and the Son and that they were separate Personages, and that the Father introduced the Son and then told the Prophet to address his question to the Son, who would give him the answer. The Prophet never would have thought of such a thing as that, had it been a fraud.

The very fact that the Prophet made that statement that he saw the Father and the Son and they were glorious Personages, and that the Father spoke to him and introduced the Son, but did not ask him what he wanted, is one of the most significant things that ever occurred in the history of this world. The Prophet, if he had been telling an untruth, even if he had thought that the Father and the Son were separate Personages, would have made another very serious error, if he had lied about it. More than likely he would have said he saw the Father and the Son and the Father asked him what he wanted, and the Father gave him the answer. It would have been fatal to his story. He did not make a mistake. It was Jesus who answered his question, and the Father introduced his Son, just as he did at the baptism of the Savior, and just as he did to the three, Peter, James, and John, on the Mount, and the Savior gave the answer, as all answers have come from our Father in heaven from the beginning, since Adam was driven out of the garden of Eden down to this day. They have all come through the Son. . . .

Do I believe that the Prophet saw the Father and the Son? I certainly do. I know it. I do not need a vision. Reason teaches that to me. And then I have that knowledge also by the guidance of the Spirit of the Lord. The Lord has made it known to me.

In Conference Report, April 1960, 71–72.

Follow Him

Our Savior, Jesus Christ, is the great Exemplar. Our mission is to pattern our lives after Him and do the things He wants us to do. " . . . what manner of men ought ye to be?" He asked His Nephite disciples, and then He answered: "Verily I say unto you, even as I am." (3 Ne. 27:27.)

I rejoice in the privilege of following in His footsteps. I am grateful for the words of eternal life which I have received, I am very glad to say, in this world, and for the hope of eternal life which is mine in the world to come if I will remain faithful and true to the end.

All my life I have studied and pondered the principles of the gospel and sought to live the laws of the Lord. As a result there has come into my heart a great love for Him and for His work and for all those who seek to further His purposes in the earth.

I know that He lives, that He rules in the heavens above and in the earth beneath, and that His purposes shall prevail. He is our Lord and our God. As He Himself said to Joseph Smith: "The Lord is God, and beside Him there is no Savior."

"I Know That My Redeemer Liveth," Ensign, *December 1971, 27.*

To Be Tried and Tested

The Savior came to earth, not alone to redeem men, but to overcome the world, to gain mortal experiences, to be tried and tested, as is the case with all of us. . . .

Christ did not study chemistry, or physics or sociology in the colleges of his day. Indeed, as we know them, these subjects were neither devised nor taught in his day.

But he did so live as to receive knowledge by revelation from the Holy Ghost, thus setting the pattern for all of us. We are commanded to seek learning, even by study and also by faith. I think we should do all we can during our student years to learn those things which will benefit us during our mortal probations and enable us to have the means and talents to further the Lord's work on earth.

Church News, *16 January 1971.*

The Lord Directs Us

I think there is one thing which we should have exceedingly clear in our minds. Neither the President of the Church, nor the First Presidency, nor the united voice of the First Presidency and the Twelve will ever lead the Saints astray or send forth counsel to the world that is contrary to the mind and will of the Lord. . . .

The Lord is with his people. The cause of righteousness shall prevail. Our cause is just, and the Lord will guide and direct us and bring us off triumphant in the end.

In Conference Report, April 1972, 99.

Twilight of Life

As I stand now, in what I might call the twilight of life, with the realization that in a not-far-distant day I shall be called upon to give an account of my mortal stewardship, I bear testimony again of the truth and divinity of this great work.

I know that God lives and that he sent his beloved Son into the world to atone for our sins.

I know that the Father and the Son appeared to the Prophet Joseph Smith to usher in this final gospel dispensation.

I know that Joseph Smith was and is a prophet; moreover, that this is the

Lord's church, and that the gospel cause shall roll forward until the knowledge of the Lord covers the earth as the waters cover the sea.

I am sure that we all love the Lord. I know that he lives, and I look forward to that day when I shall see his face, and I hope to hear his voice say unto me: "Come, ye blessed of my Father, inherit the kingdom prepared for you from the foundation of the world." (Matt. 25:34.)

In Conference Report, October 1971, 178–79.

HAROLD B. LEE

Eleventh President of The Church of Jesus Christ of Latter-day Saints

Born
28 March 1899

Ordained an Apostle
10 April 1941

Years as President
1971–1973

Died
26 December 1973, age 74

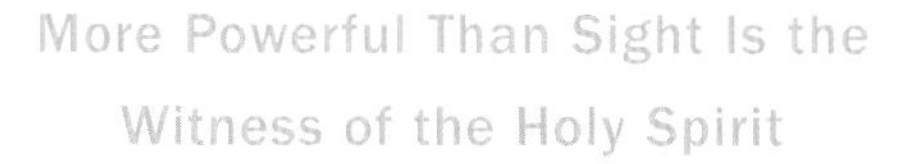

More Powerful Than Sight Is the Witness of the Holy Spirit

When I came to this position as a member of the Quorum of the Twelve, I was told that my chief responsibility now was to bear testimony of the divine mission of the Lord and Savior of the world. That was almost a crushing realization of what it meant to be a member of the Quorum of the Twelve Apostles. I was assigned to give the Easter talk the Sunday night following the general conference. As I locked myself in one of the rooms of the Church office building, I took out my Bible and read from the four Gospels the life of the Master, particularly leading down to his crucifixion and resurrection. And as I read, I became aware that something different was happening. It no longer was just a story of the doings of the Master, but I realized that I was having an awareness of something I had not had before. It seemed that I was reliving. I was feeling intently the actual experiences about which I was reading. And when I stood that Sunday night, after expressing myself as to the divine mission of the

Lord, I said, "And now, as one of the least among you, I declare with all my soul that I know . . ."

I knew with a certainty that I had never known before. Whether that was the more sure word of prophecy I had received, I don't know. But it was with such conviction! More powerful than sight is the witness of the Holy Spirit which bears testimony to your spirit that God lives, that Jesus is the Christ, that this is indeed the work of God. I knew it because I had felt it, and there had been a testimony borne to my soul that I could not deny.

"Objectives of Church Education," address to seminary leaders, Brigham Young University, 17 June 1970.

Stand at the Door

The Master said to John, "Behold, I stand at the door and knock and if any man will hear my voice and will open the door, I will come in to him and sup with him, and him with me." He would bid us all to have in mind that He is not far away. It isn't the Master who keeps Himself from us, but rather we who keep ourselves from Him. Outside of the door of our own soul He is knocking, but we have to hear His voice and we have to open the door before He can come in to help us with our problems. No person ever heard His voice, or had impressions that came from Him, except he was humble in the keeping of the commandments of God, which humility and which obedience entitled him to the companionship of the spirit by which divine truth could be revealed.

"Faith," address given at Brigham Young University, 28 June 1955, microfilm, LDS Church Archives, 1.

My Mind Was Being Directed

I was faced with a difficult, trying problem. I know what Enos means when he said, "My soul hungered, and I went out by myself where I could pray." I had a spiritual experience. I saw no light. I heard no voice to my physical senses, but I knew then as surely as I know now that I live, that on that night, when I was struggling, seeking, I had done everything in my power to prepare myself for the great responsibility that lay ahead. I knew in my own soul that that night my mind was being directed by an omnipotent power which pierced my very soul. And when I read the experience of Elijah the prophet, I knew what Elijah meant when he related his experience when the power of the Lord drew near to him.

"And he said, Go forth, and stand upon the mount before the Lord. And, behold, the Lord passed by, and a great and strong wind rent the mountains, and brake in pieces the rocks before the Lord; but the Lord was not in the wind: and after the wind an earthquake; but the Lord was not in the earthquake:

"And after the earthquake a fire; but the Lord was not in the fire: and after the fire a still small voice.

"And it was so, when Elijah heard it, that he wrapped his face in his mantle, and went out, and stood in the entering in of the cave. And, behold, there came a voice unto him, and said, What doest thou here, Elijah?" (1 Kings 19:11–13.) . . .

In all solemnity, and with all my soul, I bear you my testimony that I know that Jesus lives, that he is the Savior of the world. I know that he reveals himself and is revealing himself to his prophets. Week by week, day by day, we see the on-rolling of his works, guided and directed, and shepherded on every side, through the president of the Church, who has been set apart to preside as the mouthpiece of the Lord to His Church.

"'But Arise and Stand upon Thy Feet'—and I Will Speak with Thee," BYU Speeches of the Year, *7 February 1956, 11–12.*

Obedience to God's Will

Many times I personally have wondered at the Master's cry of anguish in the Garden of Gethsemane. "And he went a little farther, and fell on his face, and prayed, saying, O my Father, if it be possible, let this cup pass from me: nevertheless not as I will, but as thou wilt." (Matt. 26:39.)

As I advance in years, I begin to understand in some small measure how the Master must have felt. In the loneliness of a distant hotel room 2,500 miles away, you, too, may one day cry out from the depths of your soul as was my experience: "O dear God, don't let her die! I need her; her family needs her."

Neither the Master's prayer nor my prayer was answered. The purpose of that personal suffering may be only explained in what the Lord said through the Apostle Paul:

"Though he were a Son yet learned he obedience by the things which he suffered;

"And being made perfect, he became the author of eternal salvation unto all them that obey him." (Heb. 5:8–9.)

So it is in our day. God grant that you and I may learn obedience to God's will, if necessary by the things which we suffer. One of the things that characterizes us as Saints, as King Benjamin told us, was to be "submissive, meek, humble, patient, full of love, willing to submit to all things which the Lord seeth fit to inflict upon him, even as a child doth submit to his father." (Mosiah 3:19.)

In Conference Report, October 1965, 130–31.

Guide Me, O Lord

Someone asked a great surgeon, "How does it feel to have the power of life and death in your hands as you operate?" The surgeon answered, "I never feel that way. When I was a young, cocksure surgeon, I was proud of my ability and my record. Then one day I had to make a hair-breadth decision. I wasn't correct. For some time, I wouldn't operate. As I sat depressed, thinking of my failure, it suddenly came to me, in all humility, that God had given me these hands, had given me these brains, not to be wasted. I prayed to him then to let me have another chance. I still do. I pray each time I take a scalpel in hand, 'Guide my hands, O Lord, and give me of thy knowledge.' You see, he is the famous surgeon, I am only his servant."

He is also the famous architect. He is also the greatest of all teachers. Did you ever think that scientists have discovered anything that God didn't already know? Think of it. He has given you and me hands. He has given you and me brains, and he hasn't given them to us to waste. He expects us to lean on him and exercise to the best of our ability in order to use them righteously in righteous purposes. . . .

As I have sought to live as close as I know how, to know his mind and will concerning matters, and to take the first steps during this last change in the Presidency of the Church, I need your faith and prayers. . . . I plead with you to pray for me, and I promise you that I will try to so live that the Lord can answer your prayers through me. I'll try my best to be your servant.

13 August 1972 M-Men and Gleaner fireside address, Salt Lake Tabernacle, microfilm, LDS Church Archives, 1, 4.

Christ's Presence

I have an interesting session with every missionary company in the temple on the fifth floor, in the big assembly room, where they are invited to ask any questions they may wish to ask about the temple ordinances.

In one of these sessions a missionary asked, "Can you tell us a place in this temple where the Lord has appeared?" I suppose he was referring to a testimony that some have borne about someone who had appeared in the temple.

I said, "Now don't look for *a* place. This is the House of the Lord. This is where the Lord comes when he comes to see us on the earth. I imagine he has walked all the halls and every room. He is looking at us; maybe he is here today. I can't imagine a place where he would rather be than right here. Here are 300 or so of you going out on missions to preach his gospel. Maybe he is here with you."

L. Brent Goates, Harold B. Lee, Prophet and Seer *(Salt Lake City: Bookcraft, 1985), 391–92.*

I Heard a Voice

As a young boy I was out on a farm waiting for my father to finish his day's work, playing about and manufacturing things to wile away the time, when I saw over the fence in the neighbor's yard some broken-down buildings where the sheds were caving in and had rotting timbers. I imagined that that might be a castle that I should explore, so I went over to the fence and started to climb through; then I heard a voice as distinctly as you are hearing mine: "Harold, don't go over there." I looked in every direction to see where the speaker was. I wondered if it was my father, but he couldn't see me. There was no one in sight. I realized that someone was warning me of an unseen danger—whether a nest of rattlesnakes or whether the rotting timbers would fall on me and crush me, I don't know. But from that time on, I accepted without question the fact that there were processes not known to man by which we can hear voices from the unseen world, by which we can have brought to us the visitations of eternity.

In British Area General Conference Report, August 1971, 141–42.

Day by Day

I bear you my solemn witness that it is true, that the Lord is in his heavens; he is closer to us than you have any idea. You ask when the Lord gave the last revelation to this Church. The Lord is giving revelations day by day, and you will witness and look back on this period and see some of the mighty revelations the Lord has given in your day and time. To that I bear you my witness.

In Conference Report, October 1972, 131.

Become Acquainted with the Master

Before we can feel our kinship to our Savior and be influenced by his teachings in all our thoughts and deeds, we must be impressed by the reality of his existence and the divinity of his mission. . . .

One of the most beautiful pictures of the Master has come down to us in the

"I come to you today, with no shadow of doubting in my mind that I know the reality of the Person who is presiding over this Church, our Lord and Master, Jesus Christ. I know that He is. I know that He is closer to us than many times we have any idea."

"Stand Ye in Holy Places," *Ensign*, July 1973, 124.

writings of John the Beloved who was speaking both from his memories of Jesus and from a vision given him wherein the Lord appeared:

"His head and his hairs were white like wool, as white as snow. His eyes were as a flame of fire, and his feet like unto fine brass, as if they burned in a furnace; and his voice was as the sound of many waters; . . . and his countenance was as the sun shineth in its strength. And when I saw him, I fell at his feet as dead. And he laid his right hand upon me, saying, Fear not; . . . I am he that liveth and was dead." (Revelation 1:14–18.)

Suppose you try to put yourself in the place of one who had received such a visitation from a holy personage. Hardly had the sting of mourning been soothed after the death of Jesus when Mary, fearing that someone had stolen the Master's body from the tomb, was searching for him in the garden. She heard him speak her name and heard him say, "I ascend to my Father and to your Father, to my God and your God." Then she went and told Peter and the disciples as they mourned and wept, "And they, when they had heard that he was alive, and had been seen of her, believed not." After that he appeared to two of them near Emmaus in a form that they failed to recognize at first, as they walked and went into the country. (Mark 16:10–12.) He accepted their invitation to "abide with them" when it was eventide and the day was far spent. He sat at meat and gave a blessing on the bread that they ate, and their eyes opened so that they knew him. (Luke 24:29–31.) When they told their experience to the disciples their story was treated as had been the story of Mary Magdalene. He thereafter appeared to the disciples without Thomas being present and again when he was present and quieted their fears with his blessing, "Peace be unto you." Here it was that he "upbraided them with their unbelief and hardness of heart, because they believed not them which had seen him after he was risen." (Mark 16:14.) He invited them to see the prints of the nails in his hands and feet and the wound in his side and to handle him to make them sure of his reality as a tangible resurrected being. (Luke 24:37–41.) He dined on broiled fish and honeycomb with seven of his disciples on the shores of the Sea of Tiberias. After forty days he gathered them together on Mt. Olivet near Jerusalem to witness his ascension and they saw him "taken up, and a cloud received him out of their sight." (Acts 1:9.) But there remained with them the abiding memory of his last words to them, "Lo, I am with you alway, even to the end of the world." (Matt. 28:20.) They knew that he meant what he said.

His appearances to his disciples after his resurrection convinced them of his continued existence. Though they could not have him continually in sight after his ascension, there certainly was no confusion in their minds as to the reality of his existence.

And so it was with the Prophet Joseph Smith in our own day, as he declared in his own story to the world: "I had actually seen a light, and in the midst of that light I saw two Personages, and they did in reality speak to me; and though I was hated and persecuted for saying that I had seen a vision, yet it was true; and while they were persecuting me, reviling me, and speaking all manner of evil against me falsely for so saying, I was led to say in my heart: Why persecute me for telling the truth? I have actually seen a vision, and who am I that I can withstand God, or why does the world think to make me deny what I have actually seen? For I had seen a vision; I knew it, and I knew that God knew it, and I could not deny it, nether dared I do it, at least I knew that by so doing I would offend God, and come under condemnation."

After the vision left him, do you think for one moment that although he no longer continued to see the Father and the Son that he was not constantly assured amidst his persecutions and imprisonment that his Heavenly Father was mindful of his every act? With that sublime knowledge, it was only natural that as new problems presented themselves to him in carrying out instructions in the translation of the gold plates and in the setting up of the Kingdom of God on the earth as he was commanded to do, that he turned to the Lord in mighty prayer, and like the brother of Jared spoken of in the Book of Mormon,

"Having this perfect knowledge of God he could not be kept from within the veil; therefore he saw Jesus; and he did minister unto him." (Ether 3:20.) One who has such perfect knowledge would, as did the Prophet Joseph or Peter and Paul, walk daily in the company of angels and have conversation with them and receive from them such instructions and authority as are necessary to establish the great work he might be called to do.

Not many have seen the Savior face to face here in mortality, but there is no one of you who has been blessed to receive the gift of the Holy Ghost after baptism but that may have a perfect assurance of his existence as though you had seen. Indeed if you have faith in the reality of his existence even though you have not seen, as the Master implied in his statement to Thomas, that even greater is the blessing to you who "have not seen, and yet have believed" (John 20:29); for "we walk by faith not sight" (2 Cor. 5:7), although not seeing, yet believing we rejoice with joy unspeakable in receiving the end of our faith, even the salvation of our souls (1 Peter 1:8–9). The testimony of Jesus is the spirit of prophecy (Revelation 19:10), and comes only by the power of the Holy Ghost, for "no man can say that Jesus is the Lord, but by the Holy Ghost" (1 Cor. 12:3). If you have lived worthy of such a testimony you may have "a more sure word of prophecy" (2 Peter 1:19), by asking God "nothing doubting," and "by the power of the Holy Ghost, ye may know the truth of all things" (Moroni 10:5).

Decisions for Successful Living *(Salt Lake City: Deseret Book Company, 1973), 45–51.*

My Sacred Witness

I want to bear my sacred witness that because I know of the divinity of this work, I know that it will prevail; and that though there may be enemies within and without the Church who would seek to undermine and would seek to find fault and try to undermine the influence of the Church in the world, this Church will be borne off triumphantly and will stand through the test of time when all the man-made efforts and weapons forged against the Lord's word will fall by the wayside. I know that our Lord and Master Jesus Christ is the head of this Church; that He has daily communion through agencies known to Him, not only to the leaders of the Church in high positions, but also to individual members as they keep the commandments of God. To that I bear my sacred witness and leave my blessing upon all the faithful of the Church, and indeed in the world everywhere, in the name of the Lord Jesus Christ. Amen.

"Strengthen the Stakes of Zion," Ensign, *July 1973, 6.*

Testimony at the Garden Tomb

As we stood before the empty tomb in Jerusalem we, too, knew . . . [that] because of this sacrifice we, too, can have our sins remitted and be made worthy to stand in his holy presence in the days to come. . . .

I come away from some of these experiences never to feel the same again about the mission of our Lord and Savior and to have impressed upon me as I have never had it impressed before, what it means to be a special witness. I say to you with all the conviction of my soul, I know that Jesus lives. I know that he was the very Son of God.

"I Walked Today Where Jesus Walked . . . ," BYU Speeches of the Year, *10 December 1958, 12.*

He Is Close

I come to you today, with no shadow of doubting in my mind that I know the reality of the Person who is presiding over this Church, our Lord and Master, Jesus Christ. I know that He is. I know that He is closer to us than many times we have any idea. They are not an absentee Father and Lord. They are concerned about us, helping to prepare us for the advent of the Savior, whose coming certainly isn't too far away because of the signs that are becoming apparent.

"Stand Ye in Holy Places," Ensign, *July 1973, 124.*

"In all solemnity, and with all my soul, I bear you my testimony that I know that Jesus lives, that he is the Savior of the world. I know that he reveals himself and is revealing himself to his prophets. Week by week, day by day, we see the on-rolling of his works, guided and directed, and shepherded on every side, through the president of the Church, who has been set apart to preside as the mouthpiece of the Lord to His Church."

BYU Speeches of the Year,
7 February 1956, 11–12.

Soul Searching

On the day when I came to this call, which imposed a greater responsibility to be a witness of the mission of the Lord and Savior Jesus Christ—I suppose no one ever came to such a position without a lot of soul-searching, realizing his own inadequacy, and without the help of the Almighty—after a long night of searching and days of spiritual preparation that followed, I came to know as a witness more powerful than sight, until I could testify with a surety that defied all doubt, that I knew with every fiber of my soul that Jesus is the Christ, the Son of the living God, that he lived, he died, he was resurrected, and today he presides in the heavens, directing the affairs of this church, which bears his name because it preaches his doctrine. I bear that testimony humbly.

In British Area General Conference Report, August 1971, 141–42.

12

Called to Serve

I recall two or three years ago, when Brother Lee was giving his maiden address as an Apostle of the Lord Jesus Christ from this stand, he told us of his experience through the night after he had been notified of his call. I think I now know something about the experience he had. I have been going through it for twelve weeks. I believe the brethren were very kind to me in announcing my appointment when they did so that I might make the necessary adjustments in my business affairs, but perhaps they were more inspired to give me the time that I needed of a long period of purification, for in those long days and weeks I did a great deal of thinking and praying, and fasting and praying. There were conflicting thoughts that surged through my mind—seeming voices saying: "You can't do the work. You are not worthy. You have not the ability"—and always finally came the triumphant thought: "You must do the work assigned—you must make yourself able, worthy and qualified." And the battle raged on. . . .

SPENCER W. KIMBALL

Twelfth President of The Church of Jesus Christ of Latter-day Saints

Born
28 March 1895

Ordained an Apostle
7 October 1943

Years as President
1973–1985

Died
5 November 1985, age 90

When my feeling of incompetence wholly overwhelmed me, I remembered the words of Nephi when he said: " . . . I will go and do the things which the Lord hath commanded, for I know that the Lord giveth no commandments unto the children of men, save he shall prepare a way for them that they may accomplish the thing which he commandeth them." (1 Nephi 3:7.) . . . I have seen the Lord qualify men. In my Church experience I have helped to make many bishops. I have seen them grow and prosper and become great and mighty men in the Church; men who were weak and men who were foolish, and they became strong and confounded the wise, and so I rely upon that promise of the Lord that he will strengthen and empower me that I may be able to do this work to which I have been called.

In Conference Report, October 1943, 15–16, 18.

The Savior of Mankind

I read recently in a local paper of a pastor of a church in Illinois, who said that he felt the same reverence for Santa Claus that he did for Jesus Christ. He said: "I consider both of them to be folk tales, but in different categories."

He finds one difference, however; he does not question the fact that "a *man* named Jesus" did exist, and he regards Santa Claus as a "figure of the imagination."

In the magazine, *Time,* in a recent issue, a noted professor emeritus in one of our largest universities, was quoted at length on his rationalizing. To Jesus of Nazareth he gives human warmth; a great capacity for love; unusual understanding. He calls him a great humanist, a great teacher, a great dramatist. As a typical rationalization, he explains that Lazarus was not dead, but was merely " . . . brought 'back to health' by Jesus, the power of mind and learning, and by the 'therapy of his own abundant vitality!'"

I want to bear testimony today that Jesus is not only a great teacher, a great humanist, and a great dramatist, but is in very deed, the Son of the Living God, the Creator, the Redeemer of the world, the Savior of mankind. I want to testify further that he not only lived in the Meridian of Time for approximately thirty-three years, but that he lived eternities before this, and will live eternities beyond it.

In Conference Report, October 1946, 55–56.

Follow Him

The Lord is at the helm, . . . and he will continue to be there, and his work will go forward. The important question is whether we, as individuals, will be going in that same direction. It's up to us.

In Conference Report, April 1951, 104.

I Think He Smiles

In my own office at home and at the Church Office Building I have rather large pictures of Jesus as he has been portrayed by artists. I appreciate them, but they do not give me the complete or acceptable picture of the Lord, and no picture I have ever seen is adequate. I can never see the Christ with my eyes open. I must close them to get my concepts of him. . . .

I think of the Lord as he walked through Galilee and Palestine. I realize that he must have become tired and hungry and weary and thirsty, but he was ever patient. He was loving; he was kind. It seems that though it was necessary at times to rebuke people, he did what he told us in the modern revelations to do, he reproved then showed forth afterwards an increase of love toward him he had reproved (see D&C 121:43)—he had his arm around them, too. Oh how I love him for his tenderness—so forgiving, so kind.

I think of him on the cross during his great agony. He was thinking of his sweet mother down beneath him. He was tender and kind as he said to John, "Behold thy mother," and to his mother, "Woman, behold thy son!" (See John 19:26–27.) And from that hour that disciple took her into his own home.

I think of his kindness when proud and loving mothers so wanted their children to have a sight of the Master, to touch the hem of his garment, and they were pushed away—(I think of that incident at the conclusion of nearly every session of conference as we go out the back door and people crowd around to just see and speak to Christ's modern prophet—) and he said, "Suffer the little children to come unto me, and forbid them not: for of such is the kingdom of God." (Mark 10:14.)

I think of the Christ who came in our own day to the Prophet Joseph Smith and his associate in the Kirtland Temple. . . . "I am the first and the last; I am he who liveth, I am he who was slain; I am your advocate with the Father." (D&C 110:4.)

Several have said no one ever saw him laugh; however, I can imagine the Lord Jesus Christ smiling as he looked upon his people in their devotion.

Oh, I love the Lord Jesus Christ. I hope that I can show to him and manifest my sincerity and devotion. I want to live close to him. I want to be like him.

In Conference Report, April 1956, 119–20.

A Visit to the Holy Land

To visit the places where such momentous happenings affected the eternities of us all was most interesting and intriguing and added color to our picture, but we did not need to walk through the Holy Land to know eternal truth.

We realized it is not so important to know whether Mt. Hermon or Mt. Tabor was the transfiguration place but to know that on the summit of a high mountain was held a great conference of mortal and immortal beings where unspeakable things were said and authoritative keys were delivered and approval was given of the life and works of his only Begotten Son, when the voice of the Father in the overshadowing cloud said: "This is my Beloved Son, in whom I am well pleased." (Matt. 17:5.)

Not so important to know upon which great stone the Master leaned in

"I know that Jesus is the Christ, the Son of the living God. I know that. I know that the gospel which we teach is the gospel of Jesus Christ and the church to which we belong is the church of Jesus Christ; it teaches his doctrines and his policies and his programs. I know that if all of us will live the program as he has given it and will continue to give it, that all the blessings promised will be ours."

In Conference Report, October 1974, 162–63.

agonizing decision-prayers in the Garden of Gethsemane, as to know that he did in that area conclude to accept voluntarily crucifixion for our sakes. Not so needful to know on which hill his cross was planted nor in what tomb his body lay nor in which garden he met Mary, but that he did hang in voluntary physical and mental agony; that his lifeless, bloodless body did lie in the tomb into the third day as prophesied, and above all that he did emerge a resurrected perfected one—the first fruits of all men in resurrection and the author of the gospel which could give eternal life to obedient man.

Not so important to know where he was born and died and resurrected but to know for a certainty that the Eternal, Living Father came to approve his Son in his baptism and later in his ministry, that the Son of God broke the bands of death and established the exaltation, the way of life, and that we may grow like him in knowledge and perfected eternal life. And this I know and give my solemn witness.

In Conference Report, April 1961, 81.

The Savior's Example in Resisting Temptation

The importance of not accommodating temptation in the least degree is underlined by the Savior's example. Did not he recognize the danger when he was on the mountain with his fallen brother, Lucifer, being sorely tempted by that master tempter? He could have opened the door and flirted with danger by saying, "All right, Satan, I'll listen to your proposition. I need not succumb, I need not yield, I need not accept—but I'll listen."

Christ did not so rationalize. He positively and promptly closed the discussion, and commanded: "Get thee hence, Satan," meaning, likely, "Get out of my sight—get out of my presence—I will not listen—I will have nothing to do with you." Then, we read, "the devil leaveth him."

This is our proper pattern, if we would prevent sin rather than be faced with the much more difficult task of curing it. As I study the story of the Redeemer and his temptations, I am certain he spent his energies fortifying himself against temptation rather than battling with it to conquer it.

The Miracle of Forgiveness *(Salt Lake City: Bookcraft, 1969), 216–17.*

I Know That He Lives

I know that the Lord lives—that God who was with Adam, that God who came to the banks of the Jordan River to say, "This is my beloved Son, in whom I am well pleased" (Matt. 3:17), to introduce his Son to a world that was to depend so completely on him. I know that was the God that we worship, who came on the Mount of Transfiguration and said again to those servants, Peter, James, and John, who were to carry on the work of the Lord even in their imperfections: "This is my beloved Son, in whom I am well pleased" (Matt. 17:5), the same God—we know he lives and exists—who came in the state of New York and said those same things that he had already said to the Nephites—and now said to a world that had been traveling in darkness for a long, long time—"This is My Beloved Son. Hear him!" (Joseph Smith 2:17.)

I know that Jesus is the Christ, the Son of the living God. I know that. I know that the gospel which we teach is the gospel of Jesus Christ and the church to which we belong is the church of Jesus Christ; it teaches his doctrines and his policies and his programs. I know that if all of us will live the program as he has given it and will continue to give it, that all the blessings promised will be ours.

In Conference Report, October 1974, 162–63.

He Knows What He Is Doing

A prominent doctor, knowing of my surgery and cancer treatments, exhibited a little surprise at my assuming the great responsibility of the church presidency. He was not a member of the Church and evidently had never known the pull and the pressure one feels when one has a positive assurance that the Lord is *not* playing games, but rather has a serious program for man and for his glory. The Lord knows what He is doing, and all His moves are appropriate and right.

And I was surprised also that any man would wonder and question the work of the Lord. We who have the positive assurance and testimony of the divinity of this work do not question the ways or determinations of the Lord.

I know without question that God lives and have a feeling of sorrow for those people in the world who live in the gray area of doubt, who do not have such an assurance.

I know that the Lord Jesus Christ is the Only Begotten Son of our Heavenly Father, and that He assisted in the creation of man and of all that serves man, including the earth and all that is in the world. He was the Redeemer of mankind and the Savior of this world and the author of the plan of salvation. . . .

I know that the Lord has contact with His prophets, and that He reveals the truth today to His servants as He did in the days of Adam and Abraham and Moses and Peter and Joseph and the numerous others throughout time. . . .

There have been many times when man would not listen, and, of course, where there is no ear, there is no voice.

In Conference Report, October 1976, 164.

Come, Follow Me

Jesus knew who he was and why he was here on this planet. That meant he could lead from strength rather than from uncertainty or weakness. . . .

Jesus said several times, "Come, follow me." His was a program of "do what I do," rather than "do what I say." His innate brilliance would have permitted him to put on a dazzling display, but that would have left his followers far behind. He walked and worked with those he was to serve. His was not a long-distance leadership. He was not afraid of close friendships; he was not afraid that proximity to him would disappoint his followers. The leaven of true leadership cannot lift others unless we are with and serve those to be led. . . .

The Savior's leadership was selfless. He put himself and his own needs second and ministered to others beyond the call of duty, tirelessly, lovingly, effectively. So many of the problems in the world today spring from selfishness and self-centeredness in which too many make harsh demands of life and others in order to meet their demands. This is a direct reversal of the principles and practices pursued so perfectly by that perfect example of leadership, Jesus of Nazareth. . . .

Jesus had perspective about problems and people. He was able to calculate carefully at long range the effect and impact of utterances, not only on those who were to hear them at the moment, but on those who would read them 2,000 years later. So often, secular leaders rush in to solve problems by seeking to stop the present pain, and thereby create even greater difficulty and pain later on. . . .

Jesus was not afraid to make demands of those he led. His leadership was not condescending or soft. . . .

The scriptures contain many marvelous case studies of leaders who, unlike Jesus, were not perfect but were still very effective. It would do us all much good if we were to read them—and read them often. . . .

Perhaps the most important thing I can say about Jesus Christ, more important than all else I have said, is that he lives. He really does embody all those virtues and attributes the scriptures tell us of. If we can come to know that, we then know the central reality about man and the universe. If we don't accept that truth and that reality, then we will not have the fixed principles or the transcendent truths by which to live out our lives in happiness and in service. In other words, we will find it very difficult to be significant leaders unless we recognize the reality of the perfect leader, Jesus Christ, and let him be the light by which we see the way!

"Jesus: the Perfect Leader," Ensign, *August 1979, 5–7.*

"Perhaps the most important thing I can say about Jesus Christ, more important than all else I have said, is that he lives. He really does embody all those virtues and attributes the scriptures tell us of. If we can come to know that, we then know the central reality about man and the universe."

"Jesus: the Perfect Leader," *Ensign*, August 1979, 5–7.

The Lord Made It Clear

Those of us today who are sustained by you as prophets, seers, and revelators came to feel in the spring of 1978 much as the early brethren did when the revelation came to the effect "that the Gentiles should be fellowheirs . . . and partakers of his promise in Christ by the gospel" (Eph. 3:6). . . .

We had the glorious experience of having the Lord indicate clearly that the time had come when all worthy men and women everywhere can be fellow-heirs and partakers of the full blessings of the gospel. I want you to know, as a special witness of the Savior, how close I have felt to him and to our Heavenly Father as I have made numerous visits to the upper rooms in the temple, going on some days several times by myself. The Lord made it very clear to me what was to be done. We do not expect the people of the world to understand such things, for they will always be quick to assign their own reasons or to discount the divine process of revelation.

The New Era, *April 1980, 33–36.*

My Friend, My Savior, My Lord, My God

"We talk of Christ, we rejoice in Christ, we preach of Christ, we prophesy of Christ, and we write according to our prophecies, that our children may know to what source they may look for a remission of their sins." (2 Ne. 25:26.)

For the past century and a half since the Restoration, beginning with the Prophet Joseph Smith, the latter-day prophets of God have raised their voices in clarity and with authority and truth as they have borne their testimonies of the divinity of this great latter-day work and the redemptive power of the gospel of Jesus Christ.

To the testimonies of these mighty men I add my testimony. I know that Jesus Christ is the Son of the living God and that He was crucified for the sins of the world. He is my friend, my Savior, my Lord, and my God.

"The Lord Expects Righteousness," Ensign, *November 1982, 5–6.*

Simon Dewey

13

EZRA TAFT BENSON

Thirteenth President of The Church of Jesus Christ of Latter-day Saints

Born
4 August 1899

Ordained an Apostle
7 October 1943

Years as President
1985–1994

Died
30 May 1994, age 94

The Greatest Event

There is nothing in history to equal that dramatic announcement "He is not here, but is risen."

The greatest events of history are those which affect the greatest number for the longest periods. By this standard, no event could be more important to individuals or nations than the resurrection of the Master. The eventual resurrection of every soul who has lived and died on earth is a scriptural certainty. And surely there is no event for which one should make more careful preparation.

Nothing is more absolutely universal than the resurrection. Every living being will be resurrected. ". . . as in Adam all die, even so in Christ shall all be made alive" (1 Cor. 15:22). . . .

Yes, the Lord Jesus Christ liberated man from the world, by the pure gospel of love. He demonstrated that man, through a love of God, and through kindness and charity to his fellows, could achieve his highest potential. He lived the plain and sure doctrine of service, of doing good to all men, friends and enemies alike. His charge to return good for evil is still the greatest challenge to the mind of man. At the same time it is man's greatest weapon.

No other single influence has had so great an impact on this earth as the life of Jesus Christ. We cannot conceive of our lives without his teachings. Without him we would be lost in a morass of beliefs and worships born in fear and darkness, where the sensual and materialistic hold sway.

We are far short of the goal he set for us, but we must never lose sight of it. Nor must we forget that our great climb toward the light—toward perfection—would not be possible except for his teachings, his life, his death, and his resurrection. . . .

I give you my solemn witness and testimony that I know that Jesus the Christ lives. He was in very deed raised from the dead, as we shall be. He is the "resurrection and the life."

29 March 1959 Easter sunrise service address, Hollywood Bowl, California, in So Shall Ye Reap: Selected Addresses of Ezra Taft Benson, *comp. Reed A. Benson (Salt Lake City: Deseret Book Company, 1960), 4–9.*

He Will Pour out Peace

Men and women who turn their lives over to God will find out that he can make a lot more out of their lives than they can. He will deepen their joys, expand their vision, quicken their minds, strengthen their muscles, lift their spirits, multiply their blessings, increase their opportunities, comfort their souls, raise up friends, and pour out peace.

"Jesus Christ—Gifts and Expectations," in Speeches of the Year: BYU Devotional and Ten-Stake Fireside Addresses 1974–5 *(Provo: Brigham Young University Press, 1975).*

Gifts from God

I would like to talk to you about a few of the many gifts we have received from our Lord, Jesus Christ, and what we in turn might give to him.

First, he gave us the perfect model—himself—after which we are to pattern our lives. He said, "Greater love hath no man than this, that a man lay down his life for his friends" (John 15:13). Not only did he lay down before us the perfect example for earthly living, but for our sake he willingly gave us his life. He went through an agony both in body and spirit, of which we cannot comprehend, to bring to us the glorious blessing of the Atonement and the Resurrection (see D&C 19:15–19).

That man is greatest and most blessed and joyful whose life most closely fits the pattern of the Christ. This has nothing to do with earthly wealth, power, or prestige. The only true test of greatness, blessedness, joyfulness is how close a life can come to being like the Master, Jesus Christ. . . .

Secondly, . . . he has provided us the gift of a prophet. Of all mortal men, we should keep our eyes most firmly fixed on the captain, the prophet, seer, and revelator, and President of The Church of Jesus Christ of Latter-day Saints. . . . A good way to measure your standing with the Lord is to see how you feel about, and act upon, the inspired words of his earthly representative, the Prophet-President. . . .

The most important prophet, so far as we are concerned, is the one who is living in our day and age. This is the prophet who has today's instructions from God to us. God's revelation to Adam did not instruct Noah how to build the ark. . . .

Thirdly . . . is the gift of his church, The Church of Jesus Christ of Latter-day Saints, "the only true and living Church upon the face of the whole earth" (D&C 1:30). . . . It is the organized means which God is using to establish and expand his work. We must work with it and in it, build it up and move it forward. . . .

Fourthly . . . is the gift of scripture, particularly the Book of Mormon. . . .

I have noted within the Church the difference in discernment, in insight, in conviction, and in spirit between those who know and love the Book of Mormon and those who do not. That book is a great sifter.

Fifth . . . is the gift of his Constitution. The Lord said, "I established the Constitution of this land, by the hands of wise men whom I raised up" (D&C 101:80). . . .

Christ's great gift to us was his life and sacrifice—should that not then be our small gift to him—our lives and sacrifices, not only now, but in the future?

"Jesus Christ—Gifts and Expectations," in Speeches of the Year: BYU Devotional and Ten-Stake Fireside Addresses 1974–5 *(Provo: Brigham Young University Press, 1975).*

Christians?

The question is sometimes asked, "Are Mormons Christians?" We declare the divinity of Jesus Christ. We look to Him as the only source of our salvation. We strive to live His teachings, and we look forward to the time that He shall come again on this earth to rule and reign as King of Kings and Lord of Lords. In the words of a Book of Mormon prophet, we say to men today, "There [is] no other name given nor any other way nor means whereby salvation can come unto the children of men, only in and through the name of Christ, the Lord Omnipotent" (Mosiah 3:17).

The Teachings of Ezra Taft Benson *(Salt Lake City: Bookcraft, 1988), 10.*

From the Inside Out

When you choose to follow Christ, you choose to be changed. . . . The Lord works from the inside out. The world works from the outside in. The world would take people out of the slums. Christ takes the slums out of people, and then they take themselves out of the slums. The world would mold men by changing their environment. Christ changes men, who then change the environment. The world would shape human behavior, but Christ can change human nature.

"Born of God," Ensign, *November 1985, 5–6.*

"We declare the divinity of Jesus Christ. We look to Him as the only source of our salvation. We strive to live His teachings, and we look forward to the time that He shall come again on this earth to rule and reign as King of Kings and Lord of Lords."

The Teachings of Ezra Taft Benson, 10.

President Benson Shares a Story

She was a young girl. She had sacrificed her worldly plans to spend long, tedious hours in work in order to provide for and raise her younger orphan brother. But now she lay on her bed, dying of a sickness. She called for her bishop, and as she talked to him in her last moments, he held her rough, hard, work-calloused hand in his. Then she asked the question "How will God know that I am his?"

Gently he raised her wrist and answered, "Show him your hands."

Someday we may see that pair of hands that sacrificed so much for us. Are our hands clean, and do they show the signs of being in his service? Are our hearts pure and filled with his thoughts?

Each week we make a solemn covenant to be like him and take him for our leader, to always remember him in everything and keep all of his commandments. In return he promises to give us his Spirit.

"Jesus Christ—Gifts and Expectations," in Speeches of the Year: BYU Devotional and Ten-Stake Fireside Addresses 1974–5 *(Provo: Brigham Young University Press, 1975).*

A Testimony of Jesus

A testimony is one of the few possessions we may take with us when we leave this life. Let me explain what it means to have a testimony of Jesus.

To have a testimony of Jesus is to possess knowledge through the Holy Ghost of the divine mission of Jesus Christ.

A testimony of Jesus is to know the divine nature of our Lord's birth—that He is indeed the Only Begotten Son of God in the flesh.

A testimony of Jesus is to know that He was the promised Messiah and that while He sojourned among men He accomplished many mighty miracles.

A testimony of Jesus is to know that the laws He prescribed as His doctrine are true and then to abide by those laws and ordinances.

A testimony of Jesus is to know that He voluntarily took upon Himself the sins of all mankind in the Garden of Gethsemane, which caused Him to suffer in both body and spirit and to bleed from every pore. All this He did so that we would not have to suffer, if we should repent. (See Doctrine and Covenants 19:16, 18.)

A testimony of Jesus is to know that He came forth triumphantly from the grave with a physical, resurrected body. And because He lives, so shall all mankind.

A testimony of Jesus is to know that God the Father and His Son, Jesus Christ, did indeed appear to the Prophet Joseph Smith to establish a new dispensation of His gospel so that salvation may be preached to all nations before He comes.

A testimony of Jesus is to know that the church He established in the meridian of time and restored in modern times is, as the Lord has declared, "the only true and living church upon the face of the whole earth." (Doctrine and Covenants 1:30.)

A testimony of Jesus is to receive the words of His servants, the prophets, for as He has said, "Whether by mine own voice or by the voice of my servants, it is the same." (Doctrine and Covenants 1:38.)

A testimony of Jesus means that we accept the divine mission of Jesus Christ, embrace His gospel, and do His works. It means we accept the prophetic mission of Joseph Smith and his successors. . . .

To walk in the steps of Jesus is to emulate His life and to look unto Him as our source of truth and example. (John 15:5.)

Come unto Christ *(Salt Lake City: Deseret Book Company, 1983), 11–13, 37, 97.*

Mark of Divinity

Jesus' entire ministry was a mark of His divinity. He spoke as God, He acted as God, and He performed works that only God Himself can do. His works bear testimony to His divinity.

Come unto Christ*, 6–9.*

Follow the Prophet

One who rationalizes that he or she has a testimony of Jesus Christ but cannot accept direction and counsel from the leadership of His church is in a fundamentally unsound position and is in jeopardy of losing exaltation.

"Valiant in the Testimony of Jesus," Ensign, *February 1987, 2.*

Another Testament of Jesus Christ

The honest seeker after truth can gain the testimony that Jesus is the Christ as he prayerfully ponders the inspired words of the Book of Mormon.

Over one-half of all the verses in the Book of Mormon refer to our Lord. Some form of Christ's name is mentioned more frequently per verse in the Book of Mormon than even in the New Testament.

He is given over one hundred different names in the Book of Mormon. Those names have a particular significance in describing His divine nature.

Let us consider some of the attributes of our Lord, as found in the Book of Mormon, that show that Jesus is the Christ. Then let us confirm each of these attributes about Him with a brief quote from the Book of Mormon.

He is *Alive:* "The life of the world . . . a life which is endless" (Mosiah 16:9).

He is *Constant:* "The same yesterday, today, and forever" (2 Nephi 27:23).

He is the *Creator:* "He created all things, both in heaven and in earth" (Mosiah 4:9).

He is the *Exemplar:* He "set the example. . . . He said unto the children of men: Follow thou me" (2 Nephi 31:9, 10).

He is *Generous:* "He commandeth none that they shall not partake of his salvation" (2 Nephi 26:24).

He is *Godly:* He is God (see 2 Nephi 27:23).

He is *Good:* "All things which are good cometh of God" (Moroni 7:12).

He is *Gracious:* "He is full of grace" (2 Nephi 2:6).

He is the *Healer:* The "sick, and . . . afflicted with all manner of diseases . . .

devils and unclean spirits . . . were healed by the power of the Lamb of God" (1 Nephi 11:31).

He is *Holy:* "O how great the holiness of our God!" (2 Nephi 9:20.)

He is *Humble:* "He humbleth himself before the Father" (2 Nephi 31:7).

He is *Joyful:* "The Father hath given" Him a "fulness of joy" (3 Nephi 28:10).

He is our *Judge:* We "shall be brought to stand before the bar of God, to be judged of him" (Mosiah 16:10).

He is *Just:* "The judgments of God are always just" (Mosiah 29:12).

He is *Kind:* "He has loving kindness . . . towards the children of men" (1 Nephi 19:9).

He is the *Lawgiver:* He "gave the law" (3 Nephi 15:5).

He is the *Liberator:* "There is no other head whereby ye can be made free" (Mosiah 5:8).

He is the *Light:* "The light . . . of the world; yea, a light that is endless, that can never be darkened" (Mosiah 16:9).

He is *Loving:* "He loveth the world, even that he layeth down his own life" (2 Nephi 26:24).

He is the *Mediator:* "The great Mediator of all men" (2 Nephi 2:27).

He is *Merciful:* "There is a multitude of his tender mercies" (1 Nephi 8:8).

He is *Mighty:* "Mightier than all the earth" (1 Nephi 4:1).

He is *Miraculous:* A "God of miracles" (2 Nephi 27:23).

He is *Obedient:* Obedient unto the Father "in keeping his commandments" (2 Nephi 31:7).

He is *Omnipotent:* He has "all power, both in heaven and in earth" (Mosiah 4:9).

He is *Omniscient:* "The Lord knoweth all things from the beginning" (1 Nephi 9:6).

"No other single influence has had so great an impact on this earth as the life of Jesus Christ. We cannot conceive of our lives without his teachings."

So Shall Ye Reap, 4–9.

He is our *Redeemer:* "All mankind were in a lost and in a fallen state, and ever would be save they should rely on this Redeemer" (1 Nephi 10:6).

He is the *Resurrection:* He brought to pass "the resurrection of the dead, being the first that should rise" (2 Nephi 2:8).

He is *Righteous:* "His ways are righteousness forever" (2 Nephi 1:19).

He is the *Ruler:* He rules "in the heavens above and in the earth beneath" (2 Nephi 29:7).

He is our *Savior:* "There is none other name given under heaven save it be this Jesus Christ . . . whereby man can be saved" (2 Nephi 25:20).

He is *Sinless:* "He suffereth temptation, and yieldeth not to the temptation" (Mosiah 15:5).

He is *Truthful:* "A God of truth, and canst not lie" (Ether 3:12).

He is *Wise:* "He has all wisdom" (Mosiah 4:9). . . .

Those who are committed to Christ "stand as witnesses of God at all times and in all things, and in all places" that they may be in "even until death" (Mosiah 18:9). They "retain the name" of Christ "written always" in their hearts (Mosiah 5:12). They take upon themselves "the name of Christ, having a determination to serve him to the end" (Moroni 6:3).

"Come unto Christ," Ensign, *November 1987, 83–84.*

Simon Dewey

14

HOWARD W. HUNTER

Fourteenth President of The Church of Jesus Christ of Latter-day Saints

Born
14 November 1907

Ordained an Apostle
15 October 1959

Years as President
1994–1995

Died
3 March 1995, age 87

The Savior of the World

I am grateful . . . for my affiliation with a people who have a firm conviction that God lives, that Jesus is the Christ; and I bear witness to you that the story of the babe born in the manger at Bethlehem is not a myth of the past, but that Jesus, the Son of God was born of Mary into mortality; that he lived among men; that he died upon the cross and was resurrected; that he actually and truly lives today; and that he is a personal being and is the Savior of the world.

"He Lives! The Witness of Latter-day Prophets," Ensign, *March 2008*, 8.

The Divinity of Jesus Christ

During the nearly two millennia since [Jesus Christ] lived, countless thousands have admired the Lord's attributes—his kindness, generosity, mercy, and charity. His teachings have been described by one classic writer as "a great sea whose smiling surface breaks into refreshing ripples at the feet of our little ones, but into whose unfathomable depths the wisest may gaze with the shudder of amazement and the thrill of love." (Augustine, *Confessions*, xii. 140.)

Although his teachings and attributes have been of inestimable value to the human family, they must be considered as by-products of those things that really command our veneration and our worship—his atonement for our sins and his resurrection from the dead. Unfortunately, too many men have worshipped at the shrine of Christ's attributes and ethics but have denied the divinity of their Redeemer.

The Lord's invitation to follow him is extended to more persons than those who are ordained as special witnesses. The call is individual and personal, and it is compelling. We cannot stand forever between two opinions. Each of us must at some time face the crucial question: "Whom say ye that I am?" (Matt. 16:15.) Our personal salvation depends on our answer to that question and our commitment to that answer. Peter's revealed answer was "Thou art the Christ, the Son of the living God." (Matt. 16:16.) Many, many witnesses can give the identical answer by the same power, and I join with them in humble gratitude. But we must each answer the question for ourselves—if not now, then later; for at the last day, every knee shall bow and every tongue shall confess that Jesus is the Christ. Our challenge is to answer correctly and live accordingly before it is everlastingly too late.

"An Apostle's Witness of Christ," Ensign, *January 1984, 70.*

The Gift of Love

Never did the Savior give in expectation of receiving. He gave freely and lovingly, and His gifts were of inestimable value. He gave eyes to the blind, ears to the deaf, and legs to the lame; cleanliness to the unclean, wholeness to the infirm, and breath to the lifeless. His gifts were opportunity to the downtrodden, freedom to the oppressed, forgiveness to the repentant, hope to the despairing, and light in the darkness. He gave us His love, His service, and His life. And most important, He gave us and all mortals resurrection, salvation, and eternal life.

"The Gifts of Christmas," Ensign, *December 2002, 18.*

Simple Truths

Is it old-fashioned to believe in Jesus Christ, the Son of the Living God? Is it old-fashioned to believe in his atoning sacrifice and the resurrection? If it is, I declare myself to be old-fashioned and the Church to be old-fashioned. In great simplicity, the Master taught the principles of life eternal and lessons that bring happiness to those with the faith to believe.

It doesn't seem reasonable to assume the necessity of modernizing these teachings of the Master. His message concerned principles that are eternal.

That We Might Have Joy *(Salt Lake City: Deseret Book Company, 1994), 23.*

Sinless

It is important to remember that Jesus was capable of sinning, that he could have succumbed, that the plan of life and salvation could have been foiled, but that he remained true. Had there been no possibility of his yielding to the enticement of Satan, there would have been no real test, no genuine victory in the result. If he had been stripped of the faculty to sin, he would have been stripped of his very agency. It was he who had come to safeguard and ensure the agency of man. He had to retain the capacity and ability to sin had he willed so to do. . . .

He was perfect and sinless, not because he had to be, but rather because he clearly and determinedly wanted to be. As the Doctrine and Covenants records, "He suffered temptations but gave no heed unto them." (D&C 20:22.)

"The Temptations of Christ," Ensign, *November 1976, 19.*

Follow Christ

We voice again that most important question asked by the Son of God himself, the Savior of the world. To a group of disciples in the New World, a group anxious to be taught by him and even more anxious because he would soon be leaving them, he asked, "What manner of men ought ye to be?" Then in the same breath he gave this answer: "Even as I am" (3 Ne. 27:27).

The world is full of people who are willing to tell us "Do as I say." Surely we have no lack of advice givers on about every subject. But we have so few who are prepared to say, "Do as I do." And, of course, only One in human history could rightfully and properly make that declaration. History provides many examples of good men and women, but even the best of mortals are flawed in some way or another. None could serve as a perfect model nor as an infallible pattern to follow, however well-intentioned they might be.

Only Christ can be our ideal, our "bright and morning star" (Rev 22:16). Only he can say without *any* reservation, "Follow me, learn of me, do the things you have seen me do" (see Matt. 11:29; Matt. 16:24; John 4:13–14; John 6:35, 51; John 7:37; John 13:34; John 14:6; 3 Ne. 15:9; 3 Ne. 27:21).

"What Manner of Men Ought Ye to Be?" Ensign, *May 1994, 64.*

Called to Witness

Again and again during our Lord's mortal ministry he issued a call that was at once an invitation and a challenge. To Peter and his brother Andrew, Christ said, "Follow me, and I will make you fishers of men." (Matt. 4:19.) To the rich young man who asked what he must do to have eternal life, Jesus answered, "Go and sell that thou hast, and give to the poor . . . and come and follow me." (Matt. 19:21.) And to each of us Jesus says, "If any man serve me, let him follow me." (John 12:26.)

Many people have chosen to follow Christ, and we constantly pray that many more will so choose, but to a certain few of the Lord's followers the call was more specific. Luke records that after Jesus had "continued all night in prayer to God," he "called unto him his disciples: and of them he chose twelve, whom also he named apostles." (Luke 6:12, 13.)

To these chosen twelve, the call to follow Christ meant to forsake all and to physically accompany the Lord in his ministry. Their call was a privileged one. They walked and talked with the Son of God daily. They knew the Lord intimately and feasted upon his word with humble and receptive hearts. They loved him, and Jesus called them his friends. (See John 15:14, 15.)

These twelve Apostles served a vital function in the Lord's plan. They were special witnesses of the Savior's divinity and of his literal resurrection. Not only did they know him during his mortal ministry, but they communed with him after his resurrection. The resurrected Redeemer appeared in the midst of his disciples in the upper room. They handled the Lord's hands and feet and learned that Jesus was not merely a spirit but a resurrected being with flesh and bones. (See Luke 24:38, 39.)

These Apostles knew of the Lord's divinity and of his resurrection with a certainty beyond all disputation. With this knowledge, born of experience and confirmed by the Holy Ghost, they were commanded to "be witnesses unto [Christ] both in Jerusalem, and in all Judea, and in Samaria, and unto the uttermost part of the earth." (Acts 1:8.)

"An Apostle's Witness of Christ," Ensign, *January 1984, 69.*

Apostles Today

In our day the Lord has again called Apostles. These Apostles have been ordained as special witnesses of Christ in all the world. They know of the reality of Christ and his redemption with a certainty born of the Spirit. . . .

As an ordained Apostle and special witness of Christ, I give to you my solemn witness that Jesus Christ is in fact the Son of God. He is the Messiah prophetically anticipated by Old Testament prophets. He is the Hope of Israel, for whose coming the children of Abraham, Isaac, and Jacob had prayed during the long centuries of prescribed worship.

"An Apostle's Witness of Christ," Ensign, *January 1984, 69–70.*

Honored Women

Jesus, our Savior through the Atonement, demonstrated his love and concern for the women of his time. He honored the poor widow who gave two mites. He taught the woman of Samaria and revealed to her that he was the Messiah. He cast out seven devils from Mary Magdalene and forgave the woman taken in adultery. He healed the daughter of the Greek woman, he healed the woman stooped and bent for eighteen years, and he healed Peter's mother when she was sick with a fever.

He restored the dead son to his mother, the daughter of Jairus to her parents, and Lazarus to his grieving sisters, whom he counted among his closest friends. As he hung on the cross, his heart went out to his mother, and he placed her in the care of his beloved disciple, John. Women prepared his body for burial. It was Mary to whom he first appeared as the resurrected Lord, and it was she to whom he entrusted the delivery of the glorious message to his disciples that he had risen.

Is there any reason to think that he cares any less about women today? Before his ascension, he promised his disciples: "I will pray the Father, and he shall give you another Comforter. . . . I will not leave you comfortless" (John 14:16, 18). As daughters of our Heavenly Father, you also are privileged to have been given that other Comforter as well, the gift of the Holy Ghost.

"Stand Firm in the Faith," Ensign, *November 1994, 96–97.*

Pure Love

"A new commandment I give unto you," he said, "That ye love one another; . . . By this shall all men know that ye are my disciples, if ye have love one to

"It is the responsibility and joy of all men and women everywhere to "seek this Jesus of whom the prophets and apostles have [testified]" (Ether 12:41) and to have the spiritual witness of his divinity. It is the right and blessing of all who humbly seek, to hear the voice of the Holy Spirit, bearing witness of the Father and his resurrected Son."

"He Is Risen," *Ensign,* May 1988, 17.

another." (John 13:34–35.) This love that we should have for our brothers and sisters in the human family, and that Christ has for every one of us, is called charity or "the pure love of Christ." (Moro. 7:47.) It is the love that prompted the suffering and sacrifice of Christ's atonement. It is the highest pinnacle the human soul can reach and the deepest expression of the human heart. . . .

Out of the abundance of his heart, Jesus spoke to the poor, the downtrodden, the widows, the little children; to farmers and fishermen, and those who tended goats and sheep; to strangers and foreigners, the rich, the politically powerful, as well as the unfriendly Pharisees and scribes. He ministered to the poor, the hungry, the deprived, the sick. He blessed the lame, the blind, the deaf, and other people with physical disabilities. He drove out the demons and evil spirits that had caused mental or emotional illness. He purified those who were burdened with sin. He taught lessons of love and repeatedly demonstrated unselfish service to others. All were recipients of his love. All were "privileged the one like unto the other, and none [were] forbidden." (2 Ne. 26:28.) These are all expressions and examples of his unbounded charity.

"A More Excellent Way," Ensign, *May 1992, 61–62.*

Mighty Miracles

In his beloved Galilee, that familiar, favored home region of Jesus, the Son of God performed not only his first recorded miracle but went on to perform many great miracles that surely must have astonished and awed the people of Galilee who saw them. He healed a leper, cured the servant of a centurion, stilled a tempest, cast out devils, healed a paralytic, opened the eyes of the blind, and restored a young woman to life who had died.

Most of the people of his home region would not truly believe. "Is not this Joseph's son?" (Luke 4:22) they asked of Jesus, refusing to acknowledge his divine heritage. Jesus wept over these people who should have known better.

"Come unto Me," Ensign, *November 1990, 17.*

A Common Yoke

"Take my yoke upon you," he pleads. In biblical times the yoke was a device of great assistance to those who tilled the field. It allowed the strength of a second animal to be linked and coupled with the effort of a single animal, sharing and reducing the heavy labor of the plow or wagon. A burden that was overwhelming or perhaps impossible for one to bear could be equitably and comfortably borne by two bound together with a common yoke. His yoke requires a great and earnest effort, but for those who truly are converted, the yoke is easy and the burden becomes light.

Why face life's burdens alone, Christ asks, or why face them with temporal support that will quickly falter? To the heavy laden it is Christ's yoke, it is the power and peace of standing side by side with a God that will provide the support, balance, and the strength to meet our challenges and endure our tasks here in the hardpan field of mortality.

"Come unto Me," Ensign, *November 1990, 18.*

Seek Jesus

It is the responsibility and joy of all men and women everywhere to "seek this Jesus of whom the prophets and apostles have [testified]" (Ether 12:41) and to have the spiritual witness of his divinity. It is the right and blessing of all who humbly seek, to hear the voice of the Holy Spirit, bearing witness of the Father and his resurrected Son.

As one called and ordained to bear witness of the name of Jesus Christ to all the world, I testify at this Easter season that he lives. He has a glorified, immortal body of flesh and bones. He is the Only Begotten Son of the Father in the flesh. He is the Savior, the Light and Life of the world. Following his crucifixion and death, he appeared as a resurrected being to Mary, to Peter, to Paul, and to many others. He showed himself to the Nephites. He has shown himself to Joseph Smith, the boy prophet, and to many others in our dispensation.

"He Is Risen," Ensign, *May 1988, 17.*

Holy Places

I have stood in the Garden of Gethsemane on many occasions. I've contemplated in my mind the suffering, the agony of the Savior. That agony that was experienced when our Heavenly Father permitted him, in a way our minds cannot even comprehend, to take upon himself the pain and sins of all mankind. My soul was filled with sorrow as I've thought of his great sacrifice for mankind.

I've stood beneath Golgotha, the place of the skull, and contemplated the humiliation of the crucifixion which led to our Savior's mortal death, but which brought to pass his and all mankind's immortality. And again my soul has been subdued.

And I've stood in front of the garden tomb and imagined that glorious day of resurrection when the Savior emerged from the tomb alive, resurrected, immortal. In that contemplation my heart has swelled with joy.

Through these experiences I've felt to pour out my soul in thanksgiving and appreciation to our Heavenly Father for the love which he and his Son have given to us through the glorious atoning sacrifice.

"The Atonement of Jesus Christ," Mission Presidents' Seminar, Provo, Utah, 1994.

I Bear Witness

Jesus is the Beloved Son who submitted to the will of his Father by being baptized by John in the river Jordan. He was tempted of the devil in the wilderness but did not yield to the temptations. He preached the gospel, which is the power of God unto salvation, and commanded all men everywhere to repent and be baptized. He forgave sins, speaking as one having authority, and he demonstrated his power to do so by healing the lame and the halt and by opening the eyes of the blind and unstopping the ears of the deaf. He changed water to wine, calmed the troubled waters of Galilee, and walked on that same water as if on solid ground. He confounded the wicked rulers who sought his life and brought peace to troubled hearts.

Finally, he suffered in the Garden of Gethsemane and died on the cross, giving his sinless life as a ransom for every soul who enters mortality. He did in very fact rise from the dead on the third day, becoming the firstfruits of the resurrection and overcoming death.

The resurrected Lord has continued his ministry of salvation by appearing, from time to time, to mortal men chosen by God to be his witnesses, and by revealing his will through the Holy Ghost.

It is by the power of the Holy Ghost that I bear my witness. I know of Christ's reality as if I had seen with my eyes and heard with my ears. I know also that the Holy Spirit will confirm the truthfulness of my witness in the hearts of all those who listen with an ear of faith.

"An Apostle's Witness of Christ," Ensign, *January 1984, 70.*

The Prince of Peace

We are all aware of the significance that a name or title can have in describing an important office. In foretelling the birth of Christ more than 700 years before it occurred, the prophet Isaiah used titles expressing great admiration: "Wonderful, Counsellor, The mighty God, The everlasting Father" (Isa. 9:6). Isaiah also used the titles *Savior* and *Redeemer*, expressing great faith in Christ and His mission (see Isa. 45:15; Isa. 47:4; Isa. 49:26; Isa. 60:16; Isa. 63:16). One of these titles that is of particular interest in our present world is "Prince of Peace" (Isa. 9:6). "Of the increase of his government and peace there shall be no end," Isaiah declared (Isa. 9:7). What a thrilling hope for a war-weary, sin-laden world!

"The Gifts of Christmas" Ensign, *December 2002, 16.*

Simon Dewey

15

GORDON B. HINCKLEY

Fifteenth President of The Church of Jesus Christ of Latter-day Saints

Born
23 June 1910

Ordained an Apostle
30 September 1961

Years as President
1995–2008

Died
27 January 2008, age 97

The Witness of a Prophet

I know that Jesus Christ is [Heavenly Father's] Son, the Redeemer of the world, who gave His life that we might have eternal life and who rules and reigns with His Father. I know that they are individual beings, separate and distinct one from another and yet alike in form and substance and purpose. I know that it is the work of the Almighty "to bring to pass the immortality and eternal life of man" (Moses 1:39). I know that Joseph Smith was a prophet, the great Prophet of this dispensation through whom these truths have come. I know that this Church is the work of God, presided over and directed by Jesus Christ, whose holy name it bears.

"We Look to Christ," Ensign, *May 2002, 90.*

The Life of Christ

Absolutely basic to our faith is our testimony of Jesus Christ as the Son of God, who under a divine plan was born in Bethlehem of Judea. He grew in Nazareth as the carpenter's son, within Him the elements of both mortality and immortality received, respectively, from His earthly mother and His Heavenly Father. In the course of His brief earthly ministry, He walked the dusty roads of the Holy Land, healing the sick, causing the blind to see, raising the dead, teaching doctrines both transcendent and beautiful. He was, as Isaiah had prophesied, "a man of sorrows, and acquainted with grief" (Isa. 53:3). He reached out to those whose burdens were heavy and invited them to cast their burdens upon Him, declaring, "My yoke is easy, and my burden is light" (Matt. 11:30). He "went about doing good" (Acts 10:38) and was hated for it. His enemies came against Him. He was seized, tried on spurious charges, convicted to satisfy the cries of the mob, and condemned to die on Calvary's cross.

The nails pierced His hands and feet, and He hung in agony and pain, giving Himself a ransom for the sins of all men. He died crying, "Father, forgive them; for they know not what they do" (Luke 23:34).

He was buried in a borrowed tomb and on the third day rose from the grave. He came forth triumphant, in a victory over death, the firstfruits of all that slept. With His Resurrection came the promise to all men that life is everlasting, that even as in Adam all die, in Christ all are made alive (see 1 Cor. 15:20–22). Nothing in all of human history equals the wonder, the splendor, the magnitude, or the fruits of the matchless life of the Son of God, who died for each of us. He is our Savior. He is our Redeemer.

"Four Cornerstones of Faith," Ensign, *February 2004, 4.*

Testimony of God the Father

[The Sacred Grove] is reverenced by Latter-day Saints throughout the world. Here is where it all began, the miracle of this great work which has spread over the earth. This is the scene of the First Vision. It was here that God, the Eternal Father, appeared with His Beloved Son, Jesus Christ, the resurrected

Lord. The Father, pointing to His Son, said, "This is My Beloved Son. Hear Him!" (Joseph Smith—History 1:17.)

Do you realize the import of that declaration? Here was God, the Eternal Father, the Almighty, bearing testimony in words plainly spoken. No more important or compelling testimony has been given of the Risen Lord than this testimony of His own Father. . . .

Of the reality and personality of the living God and of His Son, our Redeemer, I stand as a solemn and reverent witness, speaking these words by the power of the Holy Ghost, in the sacred name of Jesus Christ.

"President Gordon B. Hinckley—The Living Christ," LDS.org.

Joseph Smith's Witness

As a Church we have critics, many of them. They say we do not believe in the traditional Christ of Christianity. There is some substance to what they say. Our faith, our knowledge is not based on ancient tradition, the creeds which came of a finite understanding and out of the almost infinite discussions of men trying to arrive at a definition of the risen Christ. Our faith, our knowledge comes of the witness of a prophet in this dispensation who saw before him the great God of the universe and His Beloved Son, the resurrected Lord Jesus Christ. They spoke to him. He spoke with Them. He testified openly, unequivocally, and unabashedly of that great vision. It was a vision of the Almighty and of the Redeemer of the world, glorious beyond our understanding but certain and unequivocating in the knowledge which it brought. It is out of that knowledge, rooted deep in the soil of modern revelation, that we, in the words of Nephi, "talk of Christ, we rejoice in Christ, we preach of Christ, we prophesy of Christ, and we write according to our prophecies, that [we and] our children may know to what source [we] may look for a remission of [our] sins" (2 Ne. 25:26).

"We Look to Christ," Ensign, *May 2002, 90–91.*

His Church

[Jesus Christ] is the chief cornerstone of the church which bears His name, The Church of Jesus Christ of Latter-day Saints. There is no other name given among men whereby we can be saved (see Acts 4:12). He is the author of our salvation, the giver of eternal life (see Heb. 5:9). There is none to equal Him. There never has been. There never will be. Thanks be to God for the gift of His Beloved Son, who gave His life that we might live and who is the chief, immovable cornerstone of our faith and His Church.

"Four Cornerstones of Faith, Ensign, *February 2004, 4–5.*

Jesus Christ Reigns

I know that I am not the head of this Church. The Lord Jesus Christ is its head. My mission, my chief responsibility, my greatest honor comes in bearing solemn testimony of His living reality. Jesus Christ is the Son of God, who condescended to come into this world of misery, struggle, and pain, to touch men's hearts for good, to teach the way of eternal life, and to give Himself as a sacrifice for the sins of all mankind. He is "King of Kings and Lord of Lords, and He shall reign forever and ever" (Handel's *Messiah*). . . . I bear solemn witness that He lives and stands on the right hand of His Father.

"Warm Messages, Festive Setting," Church News, *9 December 1995.*

The Bands of Death

I have stood at the tomb of Napoleon in Paris, at the tomb of Lenin in Moscow, and before the burial places of many others of the great leaders of the earth. In their time they commanded armies, they ruled with almost omnipotent power, their very words brought terror into the hearts of people. I have reverently walked through some of the great cemeteries of the world. I have reflected quietly and thoughtfully as I have stood in the military cemetery in Manila in the Philippines where are buried some 17,000 Americans who gave their lives in the Second

World War and where are remembered another 35,000 who died in the terrible battles of the Pacific and whose remains were never found. I have walked with reverence through the British cemetery on the outskirts of Rangoon, Burma, and noted the names of hundreds of young men who came from the villages, towns, and great cities of the British Isles and gave their lives in hot and distant places. I have strolled through old cemeteries in Asia and Europe and yet other places and reflected on the lives of those who were once buoyant and happy, who were creative and distinguished, who gave much to the world in which they lived. They have all passed into the oblivion of the grave. All who have lived upon the earth before us are now gone. They have left all behind as they have stepped over the threshold of silent death. None has escaped. All have walked their way to "the undiscovered country from whose bourn no traveler returns" (*Hamlet*, act 3, scene 1, lines 79–80). Shakespeare so described it.

But Jesus the Christ changed all that. Only a God could do what He did. He broke the bonds of death. He too had to die, but on the third day, following His burial, He rose from the grave, "the firstfruits of them that slept" (1 Cor. 15:20), and in so doing brought the blessing of the Resurrection to every one of us.

"He Is Not Here, but Is Risen," Ensign, *May 1999, 70–71.*

The Price of Victory over Death

No member of this Church must ever forget the terrible price paid by our Redeemer, who gave His life that all men might live—the agony of Gethsemane, the bitter mockery of His trial, the vicious crown of thorns tearing at His flesh, the blood cry of the mob before Pilate, the lonely burden of His heavy walk along the way to Calvary, the terrifying pain as great nails pierced His hands and feet, the fevered torture of His body as He hung that tragic day, the Son of God crying out, "Father, forgive them; for they know not what they do" (Luke 23:34).

This was the cross, the instrument of His torture, the terrible device designed to destroy the Man of Peace, the evil recompense for His miraculous work of healing the sick, of causing the blind to see, of raising the dead. This was the cross on which He hung and died on Golgotha's lonely summit.

We cannot forget that. We must never forget it, for here our Savior, our Redeemer, the Son of God, gave Himself, a vicarious sacrifice for each of us. But the gloom of that dark evening before the Jewish Sabbath, when His lifeless body was taken down and hurriedly laid in a borrowed tomb, drained away the hope of even His most ardent and knowing disciples. They were bereft, not understanding what He had told them earlier. Dead was the Messiah, in whom they believed. Gone was their Master, in whom they had placed all of their longing, their faith, their hope. He who had spoken of everlasting life, He who had raised Lazarus from the grave, now had died as surely as all men before Him had died. Now had come the end to His sorrowful, brief life. That life had been as Isaiah had long before foretold: He was "despised and rejected of men; a man of sorrows, and acquainted with grief. . . . He was wounded for our transgressions, he was bruised for our iniquities: the chastisement of our peace was upon him" (Isa. 53:3, 5). Now He was gone. . . .

Then dawned the first day of the week, the Sabbath of the Lord as we have come to know it. To those who came to the tomb, heavy with sorrow, the attending angel declared, "Why seek ye the living among the dead?" (Luke 24:5).

"He is not here: . . . he is risen, as he said" (Matt. 28:6).

Here was the greatest miracle of human history. Earlier He had told them, "I am the resurrection, and the life" (John 11:25). But they had not understood. Now they knew. He had died in misery and pain and loneliness. Now, on the third day, He arose in power and beauty and life, the firstfruits of all who slept, the assurance for men of all ages that "as in Adam all die, even so in Christ shall all be made alive" (1 Cor. 15:22).

On Calvary He was the dying Jesus. From the tomb He emerged the Living Christ. The cross had been the bitter fruit of Judas's betrayal, the summary of

"*I know that my Redeemer lives,*
Triumphant Savior, Son of God,
Victorious over pain and death,
My King, my Leader, and my Lord.
He lives, my one sure rock of faith,
The one bright hope of men on earth,
The beacon to a better way,
The light beyond the veil of death.
Oh, give me thy sweet Spirit still,
The peace that comes alone from thee,
The faith to walk the lonely road
That leads to thine eternity."

Hymns (1985), no. 135.

Peter's denial. The empty tomb now became the testimony of His divinity, the assurance of eternal life, the answer to Job's unanswered question: "If a man die, shall he live again?" (Job 14:14).

Having died, He might have been forgotten, or, at best, remembered as one of many great teachers whose lives are epitomized in a few lines in the books of history.

Now, having been resurrected, He became the Master of life. Now, with Isaiah, His disciples could sing with certain faith, "His name shall be called Wonderful, Counsellor, The mighty God, The everlasting Father, The Prince of Peace" (Isa. 9:6).

"The Symbol of Our Faith," Ensign, *April 2005, 4–5.*

His Commandments

Because our Savior lives, we do not use the symbol of His death as the symbol of our faith. But what shall we use? No sign, no work of art, no representation of form is adequate to express the glory and the wonder of the Living Christ. He told us what that symbol should be when He said, "If ye love me, keep my commandments" (John 14:15).

As His followers, we cannot do a mean or shoddy or ungracious thing without tarnishing His image. Nor can we do a good and gracious and generous act without burnishing more brightly the symbol of Him whose name we have taken upon ourselves. And so our lives must become a meaningful expression, the symbol of our declaration of our testimony of the Living Christ, the Eternal Son of the Living God.

"The Symbol of Our Faith," Ensign, *April 2005, 6.*

Jesus Is the Christ

The official name of the church is The Church of Jesus Christ of Latter-day Saints. We worship him as Lord and Savior. The Bible is our scripture. We believe that the prophets of the Old Testament who foretold the coming of the Messiah spoke under divine inspiration. We glory in the accounts of Matthew, Mark, Luke, and John, setting forth the events of the birth, ministry, death, and resurrection of the Son of God, the Only Begotten of the Father in the flesh. Like Paul of old, we are "not ashamed of the gospel of [Jesus] Christ: for it is the power of God unto salvation." (Rom. 1:16.) And like Peter, we affirm that Jesus Christ is the only name "given among men, whereby we must be saved." (See Acts 4:12.)

The Book of Mormon, which we regard as the testament of the New World, setting forth the teachings of prophets who lived anciently in this Western Hemisphere, testifies of him who was born in Bethlehem of Judea and who died on the Hill of Calvary. To a world wavering in its faith, it is another and powerful witness of the divinity of the Lord. Its very preface, written by a prophet who walked the Americas a millennium and half ago, categorically states that it was written "to the convincing of the Jew and Gentile that JESUS is the CHRIST, the ETERNAL GOD, manifesting himself unto all nations."

And in our book of modern revelation, the Doctrine and Covenants, He has declared himself in these certain words: "I am Alpha and Omega, Christ the Lord; yea, even I am he, the beginning and the end, the Redeemer of the world." (D&C 19:1.)

"The Symbol of Christ," Ensign, *May 1975, 92–93.*

Christ's Healing Power

I would that the healing power of Christ might spread over the earth and be diffused through our society and into our homes, that it might cure men's hearts of the evil and adverse elements of greed and hate and conflict. . . .

Jesus of Nazareth healed the sick among whom He moved. His regenerating power is with us today to be invoked through His holy priesthood. His divine teachings, His incomparable example, His matchless life, His all-encompassing sacrifice will bring healing to broken hearts, reconciliation to those who argue and shout, even peace to warring nations if sought with humility and forgiveness and love. . . .

I testify of Him who is the great source of healing. He is the Son of God, the Redeemer of the world, "The Sun of Righteousness," who came "with healing in his wings."

"The Healing Power of Christ," Ensign, *November 1988, 59.*

Three Distinct Beings

I believe in God the Eternal Father, and in His Son, Jesus Christ, and in the Holy Ghost.

I was baptized in the name of these three. I was married in the name of these three. I have no question concerning Their reality and Their individuality. That individuality was made apparent when Jesus was baptized by John in Jordan. There in the water stood the Son of God. His Father's voice was heard declaring His divine sonship, and the Holy Ghost was manifest in the form of a dove (see Matt. 3:16–17).

"In These Three I Believe," Ensign, *July 2006, 8.*

Belief as a Child

The earliest instance of which I have recollection of spiritual feelings was when I was about five years of age, a very small boy. I was crying from the pain of an earache. There were no wonder drugs at the time. That was 85 years ago. My mother prepared a bag of table salt and put it on the stove to warm. My father softly put his hands upon my head and gave me a blessing, rebuking the pain and the illness by authority of the holy priesthood and in the name of Jesus Christ. He then took me tenderly in his arms and placed the bag of warm salt at my ear. The pain subsided and left. I fell asleep in my father's secure embrace. As I was falling asleep, the words of his administration floated through my mind. That is the earliest remembrance I have of the exercise of the authority of the priesthood in the name of the Lord.

Later in my youth, my brother and I slept in an unheated bedroom in the winter. People thought that was good for you. Before falling into a warm bed, we knelt to say our prayers. There were expressions of simple gratitude. They concluded in the name of Jesus. The distinctive title of Christ was not used very much when we prayed in those days.

I recall jumping into my bed after I had said amen, pulling the covers up around my neck, and thinking of what I had just done in speaking to my Father in Heaven in the name of His Son. I did not have great knowledge of the gospel. But there was some kind of lingering peace and security in communing with the heavens in and through the Lord Jesus.

"My Testimony," Ensign, *May 2000, 70.*

Since Time Was Measured

It is only two millennia since the Savior walked the earth. It is a wonderful acknowledgment of His place in history that the calendar now in use throughout most of the world places His birth as the meridian of time. All that went before is reckoned back from that date. All that has happened since is measured forward from that date.

Every time anyone uses a date, he knowingly or unknowingly acknowledges the coming to earth of the Son of God. His birth, as it has been popularly determined, marks the center point of the ages, the meridian of time recognized throughout the earth. As we use these dates we pay no attention to it. But if we pause to think, we must recognize that He is the one sublime figure in all the history of the world on which our measurement of time is based.

"At the Summit of the Ages," Ensign, *November 1999, 72.*

"Nothing in all of human history equals the wonder, the splendor, the magnitude, or the fruits of the matchless life of the Son of God, who died for each of us. He is our Savior. He is our Redeemer."

Ensign, February 2004, 4.

The Polar Star

We know not what lies ahead of us. We know not what the coming days will bring. We live in a world of uncertainty. For some, there will be great accomplishment. For others, disappointment. For some, much of rejoicing and gladness, good health, and gracious living. For others, perhaps sickness and a measure of sorrow. We do not know. But one thing we do know. Like the polar star in the heavens, regardless of what the future holds, there stands the Redeemer of the world, the Son of God, certain and sure as the anchor of our immortal lives. He is the rock of our salvation, our strength, our comfort, the very focus of our faith.

"We Look to Christ," Ensign, *May 2002, 90.*

My Redeemer Lives

I know that my Redeemer lives,
Triumphant Savior, Son of God,
Victorious over pain and death,
My King, my Leader, and my Lord.
He lives, my one sure rock of faith,
The one bright hope of men on earth,
The beacon to a better way,
The light beyond the veil of death.
Oh, give me thy sweet Spirit still,
The peace that comes alone from thee,
The faith to walk the lonely road
That leads to thine eternity.

Hymns (1985), no. 135.

16

Thomas S. Monson

THOMAS S. MONSON

Sixteenth President of The Church of Jesus Christ of Latter-day Saints

Born
21 August 1927

Ordained an Apostle
10 October 1963

Years as President
2008–2018

Died
2 January 2018, age 90

I Know That My Redeemer Lives

With all my heart and the fervency of my soul, I lift up my voice in testimony as a special witness and declare that God does live. Jesus is His Son, the Only Begotten of the Father in the flesh. He is our Redeemer; He is our Mediator with the Father. He it was who died on the cross to atone for our sins. He became the firstfruits of the Resurrection. Because He died, all shall live again. "Oh, sweet the joy this sentence gives: 'I know that my Redeemer lives!'" (*Hymns*, no. 136.) May the whole world know it and live by that knowledge.

"I Know That My Redeemer Lives!" Ensign, *May 2007, 25.*

Jesus Christ Leads This Church

I know without question . . . that God lives. I testify to you that this is His work. I testify as well that our Savior Jesus Christ is at the head of this Church, which bears His name. I know that the sweetest experience in all this life is to feel His promptings as He directs us in the furtherance of His work. I felt those promptings as a young bishop, guided to the homes where there was spiritual—or perhaps temporal—want. I felt them again as a mission president in Toronto, Canada, working with wonderful missionaries who were a living witness and testimony to the world that this work is divine and that we are led by a prophet. I have felt them throughout my service in the Twelve and in the First Presidency and now as President of the Church. I testify that each one of us can feel the Lord's inspiration as we live worthily and strive to serve Him.

"Looking Back and Moving Forward," Ensign, *May 2008, 88.*

He Is Risen

With the birth of the babe in Bethlehem, there emerged a great endowment—a power stronger than weapons, a wealth more lasting than the coins of Caesar. The long-foretold promise was fulfilled; the Christ child was born.

The sacred record reveals that the boy "Jesus increased in wisdom and stature, and in favour with God and man." (Luke 2:52.) At a later time, a quiet entry records that He "went about doing good." (Acts 10:38.)

Out of Nazareth and down through the generations of time come His excellent example, His welcome words, His divine deeds. They inspire patience to endure affliction, strength to bear grief, courage to face death, and confidence to meet life. In this world of chaos, of trial, of uncertainty, never has our need for such divine guidance been more desperate.

Lessons from Nazareth, Capernaum, Jerusalem, and Galilee transcend the barriers of distance, the passage of time, the limits of understanding as they bring to troubled hearts a light and a way. . . .

That we may shoulder our sorrows, bear our burdens, and face our fears—as did our Savior—is my prayer. I know that He lives.

"Peace in Our Savior," Ensign, *June 2005, 5, 7.*

The Messiah

More than 2,000 years ago, Christ, our Savior, was born to mortal life in a stable in Bethlehem. The long-foretold Messiah had come.

There was very little written of the boyhood of Jesus. I love the passage from Luke: "And Jesus increased in wisdom and stature, and in favour with God and man." (Luke 2:52.) And from the book of Acts, there is a short phrase concerning the Savior which has a world of meaning: "[He] went about doing good." (Acts 10:38.)

He was baptized by John in the river Jordan. He called the Twelve Apostles. He blessed the sick. He caused the lame to walk, the blind to see, the deaf to hear. He even raised the dead to life. He taught, He testified, and He provided a perfect example for us to follow.

And then the mortal mission of the Savior of the world drew to its close. A last supper with His Apostles took place in an upper room. Ahead lay Gethsemane and Calvary's cross.

No mere mortal can conceive the full import of what Christ did for us in Gethsemane. He Himself later described the experience: "[The] suffering caused myself, even God, the greatest of all, to tremble because of pain, and to bleed at every pore, and to suffer both body and spirit." (D&C 19:8.)

Following the agony of Gethsemane, now drained of strength, He was seized by rough, crude hands and taken before Annas, Caiaphas, Pilate, and Herod. He was accused and cursed. Vicious blows further weakened His pain-racked body. Blood ran down His face as a cruel crown fashioned of sharp thorns was forced onto His head, piercing His brow. And then once again He was taken to Pilate, who gave in to the cries of the angry mob: "Crucify him, crucify him." (Luke 23:21.)

He was scourged with a whip into whose multiple leather strands sharp metals and bones were woven. Rising from the cruelty of the scourge, with stumbling steps He carried His own cross until He could go no farther and another shouldered the burden for Him.

Finally, on a hill called Calvary, while helpless followers looked on, His wounded body was nailed to a cross. Mercilessly He was mocked and cursed and derided. And yet He cried out, "Father, forgive them; for they know not what they do." (Luke 23:34.)

The agonizing hours passed as His life ebbed. From His parched lips came the words, "Father, into thy hands I commend my spirit: and having said thus, he gave up the ghost." (Luke 23:46.)

As the serenity and solace of a merciful death freed Him from the sorrows of mortality, He returned to the presence of His Father.

At the last moment, the Master could have turned back. But He did not. He passed beneath all things that He might save all things. His lifeless body was hurriedly but gently placed in a borrowed tomb.

No words in Christendom mean more to me than those spoken by the angel to the weeping Mary Magdalene and the other Mary when, on the first day of the week, they approached the tomb to care for the body of their Lord. Spoke the angel:

"Why seek ye the living among the dead?

"He is not here, but is risen." (Luke 24:5–6.)

"He Is Risen!" Ensign, *May 2010, 88–89.*

His Earthly Ministry

Born in a stable, cradled in a manger, [Jesus Christ] came forth from Heaven to live on earth as mortal man and to establish the kingdom of God. During His earthly ministry, He taught men the higher law. His glorious gospel reshaped the thinking of the world. He blessed the sick; He caused the lame to walk, the blind to see, the deaf to hear. He even raised the dead to life. What was the reaction to His message of mercy, His words of wisdom, His lessons of life? There were a precious few who appreciated Him. They bathed His feet. They learned His word. They followed His example.

Then there were the many who denied Him. When asked by Pilate, "What shall I do then with Jesus which is called Christ?" (Matthew 27:22.) They cried, "Crucify him." They mocked Him. They gave Him vinegar to drink. They reviled Him. They smote Him with a reed. They did spit upon Him. They crucified Him.

"The Search for Jesus," Centennial Service, Lethbridge, Alberta, Canada, 11 June 1967.

In His Shadow

Like a glowing searchlight of goodness is the life of Jesus as He ministered among men. "I am among you as he that serveth," Jesus declared as He brought strength to the limbs of the cripple, sight to the eyes of the blind, hearing to the ears of the deaf, and life to the body of the dead. (Luke 22:27.)

With the parable of the good Samaritan, the Master taught us to love our neighbors as ourselves. With His answer to the rich young ruler, He taught us to shed our selfishness. With the feeding of the 5,000, He taught us to see to the needs of others. And with the Sermon on the Mount, He taught us to seek first the kingdom of God.

In the New World, the resurrected Lord declared, "Ye know the things that ye must do in my church; for the works which ye have seen me do that shall ye also do; for that which ye have seen me do even that shall ye do." (3 Nephi 27:21.)

We bless others as we serve in the shadow of "Jesus of Nazareth . . . who went about doing good." (Acts 10:38.)

"The Savior's Call to Serve," Ensign, *August 2012, 4–5.*

On the Lord's Errand

The sweetest spirit and feeling in all of mortality is when we have an opportunity to be on the Lord's errand and to know that He has guided our footsteps.

"Guideposts for Life's Journey," BYU Devotional, 13 November 2007.

Our Mediator, Our Redeemer

It is emotionally draining for me to recount the events leading up to the Crucifixion of the Master. I cringe when I read of Pilate responding to cries of the throng: "Crucify him, crucify him." (John 19:6.) Pilate "took water, and washed his hands before the multitude, saying, I am innocent of the blood of this just person: see ye to it." (Matthew 27:24.) Jesus was mocked. He was spit upon and a crown of thorns placed upon His head. He was given vinegar to drink. They crucified Him.

His body was placed in a borrowed tomb, but no tomb could hold the body of the Lord. On the morning of the third day came the welcome message to Mary Magdalene, to Mary the mother of James, and to other women who were with them as they came to the tomb, saw the large entrance stone rolled away, and noted the tomb was empty. Two angels said to the weeping women: "Why seek ye the living among the dead? He is not here, but is risen." (Luke 24:5.)

Yes, the Lord had indeed risen. He appeared to Mary; He was seen by Cephas, or Peter, then by His brethren of the Twelve. He was seen by Joseph Smith and Sidney Rigdon, who declared: "This is the testimony, last of all, which we give of him: That he lives! For we saw him, even on the right hand of God." (D&C 76:22–23.)

Our Mediator, our Redeemer, our Brother, our Advocate with the Father died for our sins and the sins of all mankind. The Atonement of Jesus Christ is the foreordained but voluntary act of the Only Begotten Son of God. He offered His life as a redeeming ransom for us all.

His mission, His ministry among men, His teachings of truth, His acts of mercy, His unwavering love for us prompt our gratitude and warm our hearts.

"Led by Spiritual Pioneers," Ensign, *August 2006, 8.*

"With all my heart and the fervency of my soul, I lift up my voice in testimony as a special witness and declare that God does live. Jesus is His Son, the Only Begotten of the Father in the flesh. He is our Redeemer; He is our Mediator with the Father. He it was who died on the cross to atone for our sins. He became the firstfruits of the Resurrection. Because He died, all shall live again. "Oh, sweet the joy this sentence gives: 'I know that my Redeemer lives!'" (Hymns, no. 136.)"

"I Know That My Redeemer Lives!" *Ensign,* May 2007, 25.

Come, Follow Me

He taught us to pray: "Our Father which art in heaven, Hallowed be thy name. Thy kingdom come. Thy will be done in earth, as it is in heaven." (Matthew 6:9–10.)

In the garden known as Gethsemane, where His suffering was so great that blood came from His pores, He pleaded as He prayed, "Father, if thou be willing, remove this cup from me: nevertheless not my will, but thine, be done." (Luke 22:42.)

He taught us to serve: "Inasmuch as ye have done it unto one of the least of these my brethren, ye have done it unto me." (Matthew 25:40.)

He taught us to forgive: "I, the Lord, will forgive whom I will forgive, but of you it is required to forgive all men." (D&C 64:10.)

He taught us to love: "Thou shalt love the Lord thy God with all thy heart, and with all thy soul, and with all thy mind. This is the first and great commandment. And the second is like unto it, Thou shalt love thy neighbour as thyself." (Matthew 22:37–39.) . . .

He invited, "Come, follow me." (Luke 18:22.)

"Led by Spiritual Pioneers," Ensign, *August 2006, 7.*

No Room

Before we can successfully undertake a personal search for Jesus, we must first prepare time for Him in our lives and room for Him in our hearts. In these busy days there are many who have time for golf, time for shopping, time for work, time for play, but no time for Christ.

Lovely homes dot the land and provide rooms for eating, rooms for sleeping, playrooms, sewing rooms, television rooms, but no room for Christ.

Do we get a pang of conscience as we recall His own words: "Foxes have holes, and birds of the air have nests, but the Son of man hath not where to lay his head." Or do we flush with embarrassment when we remember, "And she brought forth her firstborn son, and wrapped him in swaddling clothes, and laid him in a manger; because there was no room for them in the inn." (Luke 2:7.) No room. No room. No room. Ever has it been.

"The Search for Jesus," Centennial Service, Lethbridge, Alberta, Canada, 11 June 1967.

The Lord Speaks Today

Is the voice of the Lord heard today? How does it come to man? Can your search for truth be guided by His voice? Can mine? Today, as always when the true Church of Christ is on the earth, there stands at its head a prophet. And just as the voice of the Lord came to Jeremiah, Ezekiel, and Isaiah, it has likewise come to latter-day prophets.

In Conference Report, October 1964, 18.

A Time of Testing

How grateful we should be that a wise Creator fashioned an earth and placed us here, with a veil of forgetfulness of our previous existence so that we might experience a time of testing, an opportunity to prove ourselves in order to qualify for all that God has prepared for us to receive.

Clearly, one primary purpose of our existence upon the earth is to obtain a body of flesh and bones. We have also been given the gift of agency. In a thousand ways we are privileged to choose for ourselves. Here we learn from the hard taskmaster of experience. We discern between good and evil. We differentiate as to the bitter and the sweet. We discover that there are consequences attached to our actions.

"The Race of Life," Ensign, *May 2012, 91–92.*

The Perfect Example

He demonstrated love of God by living the perfect life; by honoring the sacred mission that was His. Never was He haughty. Never was He puffed up with pride. Never was He disloyal. Ever was He humble. Ever was He sincere. Ever was He true.

Jesus, throughout His ministry, blessed the sick, restored sight to the blind, made the deaf to hear and the halt and maimed to walk. He taught forgiveness by forgiving. He taught compassion by being compassionate. He taught devotion by giving of Himself. Jesus taught by example.

Deseret Sunday School Union, 4 April 1965.

Walk with Him

As you and I walk the pathway Jesus walked, let us listen for the sound of sandaled feet. Let us reach out for the Carpenter's hand. Then we shall come to know Him. He may come to us as one unknown, without a name, as by the lakeside He came to those men who knew Him not. He speaks to us the same words, "Follow thou me," and sets us to the task which He has to fulfill for our time. He commands, and to those who obey Him, whether they be wise or simple, He will reveal Himself in the toils, the conflicts, the sufferings that they shall pass through in His fellowship; and they shall learn in their own experience who He is. (John 21:22.)

We discover He is more than the Babe in Bethlehem, more than the carpenter's son, more than the greatest teacher ever to live. We come to know Him as the Son of God. He never fashioned a statue, painted a picture, wrote a poem, or led an army. He never wore a monarch's crown or held a scepter or threw around His shoulder a purple robe. His forgiveness was unbounded, His patience inexhaustible, His courage without limit.

Jesus changed men. He changed their habits, their opinions, their ambitions. He changed their tempers, their dispositions, their natures. He changed men's hearts. . . .

Where was Peter, who had promised to die with Him and never to deny Him? The sacred record reveals, "And Peter followed him afar off, even into the palace of the high priest: and he sat with the servants, and warmed himself at the fire." (Mark 14:54.) That was the night when Peter, in fulfillment of the Master's prophecy, did indeed deny Him thrice. Amidst the pushing, the jeers, and the blows, the Lord, in the agony of His humiliation, in the majesty of His silence, turned and looked upon Peter. . . .

Then there was Saul of Tarsus, a scholar, familiar with the rabbinical writings in which certain modern scholars find such stores of treasure. For some reason, these writings did not reach Paul's need, and he kept on crying, "O wretched man that I am! who shall deliver me from the body of this death?" (Rom. 7:24.) And then one day he met Jesus, and behold, all things became new. From that day to the day of his death, Paul urged men to "put off . . . the old man" and to "put on the new man, which after God is created in righteousness and true holiness." (Eph. 4:22, 24.)

The passage of time has not altered the capacity of the Redeemer to change men's lives. As He said to the dead Lazarus, so He says to you and me: "Come forth." (John 11:43.) Come forth from the despair of doubt.

Come forth from the sorrow of sin. Come forth from the death of disbelief. Come forth to a newness of life. Come forth.

As we do, and direct our footsteps along the paths that Jesus walked, let us remember the testimony Jesus gave: "Behold, I am Jesus Christ, whom the prophets testified shall come into the world. . . . I am the light and . . . life of the world." (3 Ne. 11:10–11.) "I am the first and the last; I am he who liveth, I am he who was slain; I am your advocate with the Father." (D&C 110:4.)

To His testimony I add my witness: He lives.

"The Paths Jesus Walked," Ensign, *September 1992, 5–6.*

He Showed the Way

You may recall that Jesus filled his mind with truth; Jesus filled His life with service; Jesus filled His heart with love. When we follow that example, we shall

"Of Him who delivered each of us from endless death, I testify He is a teacher of truth—but He is more than a teacher. He is the exemplar of the perfect life—but He is more than an exemplar. He is the great physician—but He is more than a physician. He is the literal Savior of the world, the Son of God, the Prince of Peace, the Holy One of Israel, even the risen Lord."

Ensign, September 1992, 5–6.

never hear those words of rebuke that came from the parables. We shall never find that we have empty lamps. We shall never be considered unprofitable servants. We shall never determine that we have been found unfruitful in the kingdom of God. Rather, when you and I follow carefully the parts of this formula and literally fill our minds with truth, fill our lives with service, and fill our hearts with love, we may qualify to hear one day that statement of our Savior, "Well done, thou good and faithful servant: thou hast been faithful over a few things, I will make thee ruler over many things: enter thou into the joy of thy Lord" (Matthew 25:21).

"Formula for Success," Ensign, *March 1996, 6.*

Jesus Is the Son of God

For us our Heavenly Father gave His Son. For us our Elder Brother gave His life. . . .

Of Him who delivered each of us from endless death, I testify He is a teacher of truth—but He is more than a teacher. He is the exemplar of the perfect life—but He is more than an exemplar. He is the great physician—but He is more than a physician. He is the literal Savior of the world, the Son of God, the Prince of Peace, the Holy One of Israel, even the risen Lord, who declared, "I am the first and the last; I am he who liveth, I am he who was slain; I am your advocate with the Father" (D&C 110:4).

"Oh, sweet the joy this sentence gives: 'I know that my Redeemer lives!'" (*Hymns*, no. 136.) Of this I testify.

"He Is Not Here, but Is Risen," Ensign, *April 2011, 4–5.*

17

Russell M. Nelson

RUSSELL M. NELSON

Seventeenth President of The Church of Jesus Christ of Latter-day Saints

Born
9 September 1924

Ordained an Apostle
7 April 1984

Years as President
2018–Present

The Living Christ

I . . . declare that Jesus the Christ lives, that His Church has been restored to the earth, complete with His power and authority, with apostles and prophets and essential ordinances and covenants.

In a coming day the Lord will return to this Holy Land. Then "the glory of the Lord shall be revealed, and all flesh shall see it together" (Isaiah 40:5). Then He will offer these words: "I was wounded in the house of my friends. I am he who was lifted up. I am Jesus that was crucified. I am the Son of God" (Doctrine and Covenants 45:52). And then every knee will bow and every tongue confess that Jesus is the Christ.

"Special Witnesses of Christ: Jesus Is the Living Christ, Our Lord and Savior," LDS.org.

What I Know

"I have learned a lot of things in my life. . . . Nothing do I know more than I know that God is our Father and His beloved Son Jesus Christ is our Savior."

"During Rome Italy Temple Youth Devotional, President Nelson Shares 5 Things to Know, 5 Things to Do," Church News, Mar. 10, 2019.

"The Central Act of All Human History"

It is doctrinally incomplete to speak of the Lord's atoning sacrifice by shortcut phrases, such as "the Atonement" or "the enabling power of the Atonement" or "applying the Atonement" or "being strengthened by the Atonement." These expressions present a real risk of misdirecting faith by treating the *event* as if *it* had living existence and capabilities independent of our Heavenly Father and His Son, Jesus Christ.

Under the Father's great eternal plan, it is the Savior who suffered. It is the Savior who broke the bands of death. It is the Savior who paid the price for our sins and transgressions and blots them out on condition of our repentance. It is the Savior who delivers us from physical and spiritual death.

There is no amorphous entity called "the Atonement" upon which we may call for succor, healing, forgiveness, or power. Jesus Christ is the source. Sacred terms such as *Atonement* and *Resurrection* describe what the Savior did, according to the Father's plan, so that we may live with hope in this life and gain eternal life in the world to come. The Savior's atoning sacrifice—the central act of all human history—is best understood and appreciated when we expressly and clearly connect it to Him.

"Drawing the Power of Jesus Christ into Our Lives," Ensign or Liahona, May 2017.

Faith to Follow Him

As we invest time in learning about the Savior and His atoning sacrifice, we are drawn to participate in another key element to accessing His power: we choose to have faith in Him and follow Him.

True disciples of Jesus Christ are willing to stand out, speak up, and be different from the people of the world. They are undaunted, devoted, and courageous. . . . There is nothing easy or automatic about becoming such powerful disciples. Our focus must be riveted on the Savior and His gospel. It is mentally rigorous to strive to look unto Him in *every* thought. But when we do, our doubts and fears flee.

"Drawing the Power of Jesus Christ into Our Lives," Ensign or Liahona, May 2017.

Call His Church by His Name

What's in a name or, in this case, a nickname? When it comes to nicknames of the Church, such as the "LDS Church," the "Mormon Church," or the "Church of the Latter-day Saints," the most important thing *in* those names is the *absence* of the Savior's name. To remove the Lord's name from the Lord's Church is a major victory for Satan. When we *discard* the Savior's name, we are subtly *disregarding* all that Jesus Christ did for us—even His Atonement. . . .

When we omit His name from His Church, we are inadvertently removing *Him* as the central focus of our lives. . . .

If we as a people and as individuals are to have access to the power of the Atonement of Jesus Christ—to cleanse and heal us, to strengthen and magnify us, and ultimately to exalt us—we must clearly acknowledge Him as the source of that power. We can begin by calling His Church by the name He decreed. . .

So, what's in a name? When it comes to the name of the Lord's Church, the answer is "Everything!" Jesus Christ directed us to call the Church by His name because it is His Church, filled with His power.

"The Correct Name of the Church," Ensign or Liahona, Nov. 2018.

Thy Will be Done

Jesus Christ, the Savior of the world—He who ransomed us with His blood—is our Redeemer and our Exemplar. At the close of His mortal mission, He prayed that His will—as the Beloved Son—might be swallowed up in the will of the Father. In that crucial hour the Savior cried, "Father, . . . not as I will, but as thou wilt." So we should pray to God, "Thy will be done."

"Lessons from the Lord's Prayers," Ensign or Liahona, May 2009.

A True Follower

In a coming day, you will present yourself before the Savior. You will be overwhelmed to the point of tears to be in His holy presence. You will struggle to find words to thank Him for paying for your sins, for forgiving you of any unkindness toward others, for healing you from the injuries and injustices of this life.

You will thank Him for strengthening you to do the impossible, for turning your weaknesses into strengths, and for making it possible for you to live with Him and your family forever. His identity, His Atonement, and His attributes will become personal and real to you.

But you don't have to wait until then. Choose to be one of His true disciples now. Be one who truly loves Him, who truly wants to serve and lead as He did.

Russel M. Nelson, "Prophets, Leadership, and Divine Law," [worldwide devotional for young adults, Jan. 8, 2017], broadcasts.lds.org.

The Savior's Joy

Joy is powerful, and focusing on joy brings God's power into our lives. As in all things, Jesus Christ is our ultimate exemplar, "who for the joy that was set before him endured the cross." Think of that! In order for Him to endure the most excruciating experience ever endured on earth, our Savior focused on *joy*!

And what was the joy that was set before Him? Surely it included the joy of cleansing, healing, and strengthening us; the joy of paying for the sins of all who would repent; the joy of making it possible for you and me to return home—clean and worthy—to live with our Heavenly Parents and families.

"Joy and Spiritual Survival," Ensign or Liahona, Nov. 2016.

Your Heavenly Father is Counting on You

When you begin to catch even a glimpse of how your Heavenly Father sees you and what He is counting on you to do for Him, your life will never be the same.

"President Russell M. Nelson Speaks to Millennials about Being Happy," Church News, Feb. 23, 2018.

The Book of Mormon is True

The Book of Mormon is a gift from God to the entire world! It was written by ancient prophets for us who live in these latter days. It is the only book that the Lord Himself has testified to be true.

The Book of Mormon teaches us about the remarkable promises God made long ago that can bless each of us in our day and continue to bless us throughout all time. Yes, these promises are available to you!

The more I study the Book of Mormon, the more I marvel at the miracle it is—how it was translated by the gift and power of God. Its central message is that Jesus Christ is the Savior of the world. It has converting power. Its truths draw every earnest seeker closer to God and fill each with a desire to know more about the restored gospel of Jesus Christ.

"Russel M Nelson's Facebook page, posted Feb. 11, 2019, https://www.facebook.com/lds.russell.m.nelson/.

Made Holy by Him

Have you ever wondered why the Lord chose to accomplish His mortal ministry in the exact location that He did? He created the earth. In His divine role, He could have selected any portion of this bounteous planet to accomplish

His mission. He could have selected the beautiful islands of the sea with their lush vegetation and breathtaking beauty. He could have chosen the scenery of Switzerland or Scandinavia, or He could have preferred to walk upon the acres of Africa and Australia.

Instead, He selected the land with places stark and arid, but made holy by His presence there. He did so for many reasons, including His desire to teach with geographical visual aids, and to fulfill scriptural prophecy.

[He chose] a land where nomads dwell, living in tents and wandering as freely as the sheep and goats that they tend. He chose to be born in Bethlehem, adjoining Jerusalem. This He did to teach symbolically and to fulfill scriptural prophecy. Years before this event the prophet Micah foretold:

"But thou, Bethlehem . . . though thou be little among the thousands of Judah, yet out of thee shall he come forth unto me that is to be ruler in Israel; whose goings forth have been from of old, from everlasting." (Micah 5:2) . . .

Why Bethlehem? Is there symbolic significance in the meaning of the name *Bethlehem*, which in Hebrew mean "house of bread"? The Great Provider declared Himself to be the "bread of life." (See John 6:48.) How appropriate it was that He, the "bread of life," was to come from the "house of bread."

But why among the animals? He, whom John declared to be the "Lamb of God" (John 1:29), was born during the season of Passover amongst the animals, as were other lambs being prepared for Paschal sacrifice.

At the birth of Him who is called the "good shepherd" (John 10:14), shepherds were the first to receive the announcement of His holy birth (see Luke 2:8–16).

At the birth of Him who once identified Himself as the "bright and morning star" (Rev. 22:16), a new star appeared in the heavens (see Matt. 2:2; 3 Ne. 1:21). Shining brightly over Bethlehem, that star had been placed in orbit far in advance of the foretold event in order that its light could coincide both in time and place with His blessed birth.

"In a coming day, you will present yourself before the Savior. You will be overwhelmed to the point of tears to be in His holy presence. You will struggle to find words to thank Him for paying for your sins, for forgiving you of any unkindness toward others, for healing you from the injuries and injustices of this life. You will thank Him for strengthening you to do the impossible, for turning your weaknesses into strengths, and for making it possible for you to live with Him and your family forever. His identity, His Atonement, and His attributes will become personal and real to you."

"Prophets, Leadership, and Divine Law," [worldwide devotional for young adults, Jan. 8, 2017], broadcasts.lds.org.

At the arrival of Him who is called "the light of the world" (John 8:12), darkness was banished as a sign of His holy birth (see 3 Ne. 1:15, 19). He was born the Son of God and the Son of a virgin mother, as foretold by Isaiah (see Isa. 7:14) and other prophets. (See 1 Ne. 11:13–21; Alma 7:9–10).

"Why This Holy Land?" Ensign, Dec. 1989.

Jesus Laid Down His Life

Born of a mortal mother and an immortal Father, he was the only one who could voluntarily lay down his life and take it up again. The glorious consequences of his Atonement were infinite and eternal. He took the sting out of death and made temporary the grief of the grave. His responsibility for the Atonement was known even before the Creation and the Fall. Not only was it to provide for the resurrection and immortality of all humankind, it was to enable us to be forgiven of our sins—upon conditions established by him. And his Atonement opened the way by which we could be united with him and with our families eternally. This prospect we esteem as eternal life—the greatest gift of God to man.

No one else could effect the Atonement. No other person, even of the greatest wealth and power, could ever save one soul—not even his own. And no other individual will be required or permitted to shed blood for the eternal salvation of another human being. Jesus did it "once for all."

"Gratitude for the Mission and Ministry of Jesus Christ," Brigham Young University devotional, Aug. 18, 1998; speeches.byu.edu.

The Same Message as Apostles of Old

The Savior stands at the head of The Church of Jesus Christ of Latter-day Saints. As modern-day Apostles of Jesus Christ, the message we share today is the same message that Apostles shared long ago—that God lives and that Jesus is the Christ.

As one of His special witnesses, I testify that because the Savior offered Himself as the infinite Atonement, you and I have the opportunity—the privilege—to be forgiven when we repent. We can also turn to Him for healing of our hearts, for strength when we are weak, and for help to do things we simply cannot do on our own. He taught us how to love, how to pray, how to endure. There's no trial we can endure that He doesn't know about. He gives each one of us hope.

I am honored to be listed among the many who teach and testify of the Lord Jesus Christ. He is the Savior of the world, and He has given us an example by which we can live.

"Rome Temple a 'hinge-point' in Latter-day Saint history, President Nelson says as he leaves Italy," Deseret News, Mar. 11, 2019.

What God Can Do for His Children

As a young surgical resident at the University of Minnesota Hospitals in the early 1950s, I was on the research team that built the heart-lung machine that allowed the first surgical access to the open, beating human heart. Working alongside brilliant minds (there and elsewhere) was exhilarating. But human intelligence has its limits. As a surgeon, I repaired hundreds of hearts. But my skills could not heal heartache, or erase grief, or salve emotional wounds. Nothing man-made can ever approach what God can do for His children.

The most able minds cannot offer redemption from sin or heal our hearts from emotional pain. They cannot generate enduring hope or joy. They cannot promise life after death or the potential of being with our loved ones beyond the grave. They cannot generate peace of mind.

But God can. Our spiritual DNA is His DNA. If our hearts are open to Him—if we believe in the divinity of the Father and His Son—we can rise from the ashes of our lives and become the men and women we were sent to earth to become.

"The most able minds cannot offer redemption from sin or heal our hearts from emotional pain. They cannot generate enduring hope or joy. They cannot promise life after death or the potential of being with our loved ones beyond the grave. They cannot generate peace of mind. But God can."

"Why have faith now? LDS President Russell M. Nelson explains during Phoenix-area visit," article from The Republic, as posted on azcentral.com, Feb. 10, 2019.

After three decades of doing cardiac surgery around the world, I thought I knew a little something about repairing hearts. Then I was called as an Apostle of the Lord Jesus Christ. In that moment, my focus shifted instantly to healing hearts another way—by turning all who will listen to the Master Healer, Jesus Christ.

"Why have faith now? LDS President Russell M. Nelson explains during Phoenix-area visit," article from The Republic, as posted on azcentral.com, Feb. 10, 2019.

I Testify of Jesus Christ

I testify that Jesus is the Christ, the Son of the Living God. He is our Creator, Savior and Redeemer, Advocate with the Father, Deliverer, and Jehovah of the Old Testament. He is the promised Immanuel, the anointed Messiah, and our great Exemplar. One day He will return to rule and reign as King of kings and Lord of lords. Eventually, we will each stand before Him at judgment day. I pray for each of us that our individual faith in Him will be acceptable.

"Faith in Jesus Christ," Ensign, Mar. 2008.

About Heidi Swinton

Heidi S. Swinton is an award-winning author and screenwriter whose works include the official biography of President Thomas S. Monson, *To the Rescue*. She has also written the PBS documentaries *Joseph Smith: American Prophet*; *Sweetwater Rescue*; *Sacred Stone*; *American Prophet: The Story of Joseph Smith*; *Trail of Hope*; and *America's Choir*. She has served on the Relief Society general board and as a member of Church writing committees. She has served with her husband, Jeffrey C. Swinton, as he presided over the England London South Mission (2006–2009) and as he served as the Director of the Laie Hawaii Temple Visitors' Center (2016–2018). They are the parents of five sons, four living, and have four daughters-in-law and thirteen grandchildren.

Image Credits

Page vi: *From Darkness to Light*

Page x: *I Am the Way*

Page 14: *Prince of Peace*

Page 28: *Holy One of Israel*

Page 42: O My *Father*

Page 56: *He Lives*

Page 68: *I Am*

Page 82: *Fishers of Men*

Page 96: *Divine Redeemer*

Page 110: *The Good Shepherd*

Page 122: *The Last Supper*

Page 134: *Living Water*

Page 148: *Light and Truth*

Page 160: *In the Shepherd's Care*

Page 172: *Why Weepest Thou?*

Page 184: *The Dawning of a Brighter Day*

Page 198: *Lead, Kindly Light*

Page 212: *As I Have Loved You*

Prophet portraits courtesy LDS Church History Museum.

Page 1: Joseph Smith, by Dan Weggeland

Page 15: Brigham Young, by Dan Weggeland

Page 29: John Taylor, by A. Westwood

Page 43: Wilford Woodruff, by Lewis Ramsey

Page 57: Lorenzo Snow, by Lewis Ramsey

Page 69: Joseph F. Smith, by John W. Clawson

Page 83: Heber J. Grant, by Lee Green Richards

Page 97: George Albert Smith, by Lee Green Richards

Page 111: David O. McKay, by Alvin Gittens

Page 123: Joseph Fielding Smith, by Shauna Clinger

Page 135: Harold B. Lee, by Knud Edsberg

Page 149: Spencer W. Kimball, by Judith Mehr

Page 161: Ezra Taft Benson, by Knud Edsberg

Page 173: Howard W. Hunter, by William Whitaker

Page 185: Gordon B. Hinckley, by Judith Mehr

Page 199: Thomas S. Monson, by Ken Corbett. Used by permission

Page 213: Russell M. Nelson, by Brendan Clary